NEWCASTLE
AND THE
RIVER TYNE

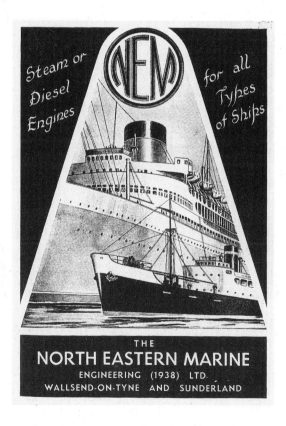

Steam or Diesel Engines — for all Types of Ships

THE
NORTH EASTERN MARINE
ENGINEERING (1938) LTD.
WALLSEND-ON-TYNE AND SUNDERLAND

A classic view showing an ancient Newcastle Quayside in quiet mood in April 1959. *JJ*

NEWCASTLE
AND THE
RIVER TYNE

*'No English river is at all comparable to the Tyne in the evidences
which it everywhere thrusts forward of the part which it played in
the industrial development of these islands.'*
W. E. Gladstone

Ken Groundwater

• MARITIME HERITAGE •
from
The NOSTALGIA Collection

First edition published in May 1990
New enlarged edition first published
December 1998

British Library Cataloguing in Publication Data

A catalogue record for this book is available from the British Library

ISBN 1 85794 105 5

Silver Link Publishing Ltd
The Trundle, Ringstead Road
Great Addington, Kettering
Northants NN14 4BW

Photographic credits: *GL* is Gateshead Library; *JJ* is John Johnson; *JR* is James Riddell; *NCL* is Newcastle Central Library; *NM* is Norman McCord; *NSL* is North Shields Library; *SSG* is the *South Shields Gazette*; *SSL* is South Shields Library; *UN* is University of Newcastle upon Tyne; and those credited *KG* are the author's.

Printed and bound in Great Britain

A Silver Link book
from
The NOSTALGIA *Collection*

BIBLIOGRAPHY

Blake, J. B. *Medieval Coal Trade of NE England* (1967)

Buswell, R. J., & Barke, M. *200 Years of Change in a 900 year old City* (Geographical Magazine, No 53, 1980)
Newcastle's Changing Map (Newcastle upon Tyne City Library, 1992)

Charleton, R. J. *The History of Newcastle* (1885)

Chatterton, K. *Ships and Ways of the Days* (1913)

Chesterton, D. R., & Fenton, R. S. *Gas & Electric Colliers* (1984)

Clarke, J. F. *A Century of Service to Engineering & Shipbuilding: A centenary history of the North East Institute of Engineers & Shipbuilders, 1884-1984* (1984)
Power on Land and Sea: A history of R.& W. Hawthorn Leslie (no date)

Cromar P. *The Coal Industry of Tyneside, 1771-1800: Oligopoly & spatial change* (Economic Geography, No 53, 1977)

Crumlin Pederson, O. *The Viking Ships of Roskilde: Aspects of the history of wooden shipbuilding* (National Maritime Museum, 1970)

Dougan, D. *The History of North East Shipbuilding* (1968)

Finch, R. *Coals from Newcastle* (Terence Dalton, 1973)

Fordyce, W. *Charts of the River Tyne* (1846)

Flagg, A. *The History of Shipbuilding in South Shields* (1979)

Fraser, C. M. *The Pattern of Trade in North East England 1265-1350* (Northern History, No 4, 1969)

Guthrie, J. *The River Tyne: Its history & resources* (1880)

Johnson, R. W. *The Making of the Tyne* (1895)

McCord, N. *Essays in Tyneside Labour History* (1978)

Martin, S. B., & McCord, N. *The Steamship Bedlington 1841-1854* (Maritime History, Vol 1, 1971)

Moir, D. M. *The Birth & History of Trinity House, Newcastle* (1958)

Newcastle upon Tyne City Council *Regeneration of the Quayside* (1980)

Newcastle upon Tyne City Library *Pottery Bank People* (1989)

O'Brien, C., & McCombie, G. *Newcastle Quayside Archaeological Report* (Archaeological Unit for NE England, University of Newcastle, 1983)

O'Brien, C., et al *Excavations at Newcastle Quayside/The Origins of the Newcastle Quayside* (Society of Antiquaries, Newcastle, 1988)

Palmer, W. J. *The Tyne & its Tributaries* (1882)

Rae, I., & Smith, K. *Built with Pride: Tyne Ships 1969-1994* (Newcastle upon Tyne City Library, 1995)

Runciman, W. *Collier Brigs and their Sailors* (reprint 1971)

Sargeant, A. J. *The Tyne* (Geographical Journal, No 40, 1912)

Smith, R. *Sea Coal for London* (1961)

Turnbull, L. *Discovering your Neighbourhood: Bill Quay* (Gateshead MBC Dept of Education (no date)

Viall, H. *Tyne Keels* (Mariners' Mirror, Vol 28)

Welford, R. *History of Newcastle & Gateshead in the 14th, 15th, 16th & 17th Centuries* (1886-7)

Willans, T. S. *English Coasting Trade, 1600-1750* (1938)

. . .and many entertaining 'Waterfront' articles over the years from the *South Shields Gazette*.

CONTENTS

ACKNOWLEDGEMENTS

My thanks for both this new enlarged edition and the first edition go to George Scott, Ron French, Ian Rae, Tony Smith and Cliff Parsons for the time they gave to research individual subjects; Roger Woodcock, Keith Byass and Laurence Dunn for supplying excellent prints; and the following for specialist information: Tony Wickens, Phil Atkins, Joe Clarke, and Norman McCord.

Thanks also to my old school friend Paul Hood for introducing me to so many knowledgeable World Ship Society people, and to Alan R. Thompson and Trevor Ermel, who not only produced excellent prints but also exceeded my requests in a unselfish fashion not often found today.

Without the help of our excellent local library staff it would be difficult to succeed in such a venture. These include South Shields, Newcastle City and Gateshead Central Libraries. Please use your library – we would certainly miss them if they went, and their combined generosity and encouragement is legion.

Bob Laidlaw, commercial artist and maths entrepreneur, drew the maps, and Tim Stephenson did some hot key work – thanks Tim! I reserve my last thanks for these true Tynesiders who 'live' this area, John Dawson, William Purvis and Eddie Spouse, for reading over the raw captions – in my case a rotten job! The last word goes to 'Mr South Shields' – John Johnson. John's generosity with his precious negatives was beyond words. As can be seen, John's contribution is the majority of pictures.

Above Thought to be *circa* 1880, 'somewhere on the Tyne', a collier brig – one of the Geordie hordes that regularly invaded the Pool of London – is well supported by two steam paddle tugs, out in mid-stream, one of which is recognised as the *Liberty*; she may well be awaiting receipt of the coal loads in the foreground.

This photograph gives a fascinating glimpse of the older-style wherries in loaded conditions: one with its 'greedy boards' (timber walls) high, the other with a level load but clearly showing the hand rudder. Other items of interest include the irons – for breaking up packed coal – and the small raised carving on the bow of the wherry. GL

Left A poignant reminder of the little boats that once swarmed over the river for more than 300 years forming the back-bone of trading. They went unacknowledged by those glimpsing the river scene before moving on, and few noticed their reduction in numbers – until it was too late! Descendants of the keelboat age and of the clinker-built inheritance from our Norse neighbours, those remaining were thrown up into a heap to 'tidy the river'! They lay rotting from about 1969 to 1976 when clearance was completed before preservation could take place. We have Norman McCord to thank for capturing this last record at Newburn. NM

INTRODUCTION: COALS FROM NEWCASTLE

We are aiming in these pages to illustrate the special characteristics of the Tyne and inevitably her relationship with coal – once our staple product. However, the association with a myriad other commercial tentacles is impossible to ignore, for it shows how each peripheral industry prospered and gave an army of Tynesiders generations of river-based employment. But it is sobering to remember these words by the Tyne's first historian, R. W. Johnson, who, as far back as 1890, gave a caution that has proved true recently, not for the diminishing coal stocks to which he then alluded, but for our once unshakable shipbuilding industry: '. . .the day of good things is short and the harvest of the Tyne must be reaped quickly, for competition began his reign in this land today. . .'

Let us briefly retrace our steps to where it all began and why. The river's shipbuilding career grew from the need to provide quick and cheap transport for coal to a burgeoning 12th-century London. Why Northern coal? Astonishingly, because the North East was the only area in Britain at that time that had the resources available for coal transportation over the distance and in the quantities required. We had the ships!

Our heritage from our Norse neighbours seems certain now to have influenced this lead, and it is believed that Tynesiders were quick to understand the meaning of relics found upon our shores long after the longboats had departed.

Undoubtedly the sea was the best way of transporting coal north-to-south, for the turnpike roads of England hadn't reached the standards needed to withstand the constant hammering inflicted by coal carts upon already limited pathways. At about the same time (around the 17th century) the coming of 'ways of rail' was still some way off. The pit-owners therefore had no

choice but to send coal vessels to London, but conditions were difficult – not everything was yet in place for the Industrial Revolution!

'The bigger colliers were usually destined for the Thames, two hundred years ago not the deep uncluttered waterway of today and where a shelf above Woolwich gave only a minimum nine feet of water, but nevertheless a river capable of floating the deepest draught merchantman to at least that point. On the outward voyage the Tyne bar also enforced limitations of size to colliers for the channel was only 40 yards wide and it was the custom to lay-up in Winter when the dangers were at their worst. . .' (J. F. Clarke, *A Century of Engineering and Shipbuilding*)

The Monks at Tynemouth, who went down to their beach 'haven' below the priory (see the map on page 116) in the 12th century to pick 'seacole' could scarcely have appreciated how great a catalyst they were to world power. They eventually needed Royal Assent for this occupation, demonstrating some early wisdom as to its ultimate importance and value, for their back-yard finance supplement became the single biggest employer this country has ever known, reaching its height in the 1920s with a million people involved in coal production in some way.

Development beyond medieval times was initially slow as wars and governments came and went, but from the 17th century, and with the coming of small staith-like structures or coal-drops, the business of transporting minerals from Tyne to Thames made rapid progress. Soon the scene was set for the North East to spawn what became the largest collier fleet based upon one river – the Tyne collier-brig was born and reigned supreme in the Pool of London with all the resemblance of a black armada! This Geordie fleet became the biggest single group of coordinated shipping ever seen around these shores, and in consequence was also a prime target of press gangs – but that's another story.

London found the produce from the Northern coalfield ideal for its uses and clambered for more of this 'Wallsend Sun'. ('The best sun we have is made of Newcastle coal,' said Horace Walpole on 17 June 1768).

The first physical restraint to the continuous supply was the coal-line receding away from the river-bank. It must be remembered that at this time it was essentially an open-cast coal-picking job (only a slight manpower development upon the few monks of Tynemouth), and the source was moving further and further from the shore; thus inevitably overland transport became an issue.

For over 100 years thereafter horses hauled crude chaldron wagons – about the same size as a modern-day medium-sized skip – from pit to riverside, and their mud paths stretched further and further back as coal 'winning' became more difficult.

Enter railways in the form of wooden wagon guides sunk into cart tracks, allowing the process to continue at a rate that just about kept up with southern demand. Evolution, or in this case demand, having been the mother of invention, Tyneside was saved, for almost certainly London would have looked elsewhere and South Wales was catching up!

Two major consequences of these almost insidious changes were to be the precursors of a Tyne revolution. The most important issue concerned navigating the still shallow upper Tyne. It was costly and frustrating for the waiting collier managers as coal delivery to the riverside coal storage areas became more and more unpredictable, tides were missed and a day added. The river became an angry bottleneck for operators.

Second, the receding coal-line meant that shorter leads to the river became desirable. An example of this was that Dunston Staiths was not as convenient (due to path deterioration) as, say, Blaydon Staiths for the coal 'won' in north-west Durham.

What happened next was that smaller craft needed to go higher up river to bring the mineral down to waiting sea-going vessels. Things would have to change, and rapidly, or the golden goose

would becoming strangulated by a serious hiatus! As Johnson said, '. . . the natural blessing of coal did not extend to the natural shape of the river. . .'

Johnson goes on to paint a picture of the early Tyne and its limitations:

'It was a tortuous, shallow stream, full of sandbanks and eccentric eddies, which, at Newcastle, men might ford at low tide. It wended its peaceful course from the junction of the North and South Tyne above Hexham through a charming valley . . . meandering by Stephenson's lonely cottage near Wylam, between the drooping willows of Ryton, doubling round Newburnhaugh and stealing with quickened force on either side of the King's Meadow [an island off Dunston] the rustic river sped on untrammelled and unstained till its waters darkened under the shadow of Newcastle Town. But even here, though deeper of hue and enslaved to the service of man, its wayward course was unfettered still. The Tyne, over what was then its navigable reach, twisted, turned, and expanded, now rushing with impetuous haste past the mid-stream projection of Bill Point . . . stretching its expanse over the marshes of Jarrow Slake, only to gather fresh force for the sweep around Whitehill Point and the final charge through the "narrows" at Shields into the broad sea beyond. . .'

Coal had nevertheless been making the journey from at least 1620 under the guidance of men who had learned how to navigate around shifting sand banks. They were also already experienced in night navigation by dim landmarks and lights through the fog on the Tyne. It was in such conditions as these that life on the river rolled on for another 200 years and may never have seen change had it not been for the dogged persistence of liberal-thinking radicals and fearless campaigners who were persecuted for their sin of speaking out against the monopolising greed of the city fathers, revealing how they intended to fight '. . .the illegal oppressions and arbitrary exactions, barbourous murthers, practised and committed by magistrates of Newcastle, both upon their neighbours and the free people of this nation. . .'

It still took another 50 years of haggling before

the River Tyne Improvement Act took effect and finally opened the way to common prosperity via the spirit of free enterprise.

We can get some idea from the aerial pictures within, showing the final shape of today's Tyne, just how much energy and enthusiasm was needed by the Tyne Improvement Committee to carve out the neat profile, docks, ports and basins that made the river such a significant force, not just in the prosperity of this country but also for that of the entire world via the influence of the old Empire.

Today, the forest of masts common in the late 19th century has gone, together with the steel-walled cargo ships of the mid-20th century. Also gone are the impatient 'flat-iron' colliers of the Thames and our own ash-hoppers – named after famous local characters and so familiar a sight as once to be thought of with contempt, but all now fondly remembered.

To understand just a little of the pride felt by local people for their evolving Tyne and the first gargantuan works, let us briefly hark back to some contemporary waxings. R. J. Charleton, in *The History of Newcastle*, looks back from 1883:

'. . . going back to 1750 we find great excitement . . . on the occasion of the launch of the *Russell* from Mr Headlam's yard. She was a fine vessel capable of carrying 30 keels of coal and the largest ship built on the river. Then in 1753, we read how the *Experiment*, built by subscribers to a West Indian trade, came back from her first voyage . . . with a cargo of sugar, rum, and coffee in return for the commodities of Newcastle. . .'

He continues:

'. . .Its banks from Scotswood to the sea resound with the din of the riveters' hammer. Shipyards are to be seen at every bend and on both sides . . . their number is rapidly increasing. The produce of the Tyne in 1882 was 133 steamers and 7 sailing vessels . . . it is pleasant to look upon these labours, and to see that they have made the Tyne of the present day one of the chief ports of Gt Britain.'

When time travel is perfected it would certainly be astounding to visit 1883!

Our nostalgic journey down through the past along this historic waterway will progress in stages from west to east. The river maps do not purport to represent exactly the industrial sites in size or location, but are included to convey their presence in relationship to the main river activity and to give a feeling of the scale of things. We have not attempted to show all riverside activity at the turn of the century, as this would be very complex at this scale, and was in any event a rapidly changing picture. We therefore apologise if you fail to find your great grandfather's glue factory, or a distant relative's alkali works! It is hoped that one day someone will produce the definitive location history of Tyneside's old industrial face through the ages.

Each geographical chapter is accompanied by a short synopsis, in which I attempt to give you at least a bit of a feeling for the main attributes of that section of the river. These represent a very personal view, intended as a precursor to the illustrations.

A note on the new edition

Although the first edition commented on a river very much in decline, the underlying message in 1990 was optimism and that perhaps the worst was over. Swan Hunter Shipbuilding Ltd was at least still building and was ever hopeful of winning new orders to continue the traditions.

However, in May 1993 the receivers were called in after the yard failed to win the order for a naval helicopter carrier – HMS *Ocean*.

Swans closed down after the completion of Type 23 frigate HMS *Richmond* on 3 November 1994 amid a political furore with claims and counter-claims ping-ponging back and forth between local MPs and the Government of the day. Between that May and November 1994 Tyneside moved in numb disbelief and over 2,000 shipbuilders were called in to receive their last pay. A Tyne without shipbuilding?

From the mid-1960s Swans had merged with many famous yards – including big names like Readhead of South Shields, Hawthorn Leslie and Vickers-Armstrong – and remained as the dominant driving force to progress a new-look campaign for orders. Nationalisation in 1977 and re-privatisation in 1985 left the group streamlined and the workforce slightly bewildered by the changes, but nevertheless focused and willing. By 1989, as the first edition went to press, Swans' Wallsend yard was the only remaining launch pad for new shipping left on the river.

A final telling comment that perhaps encapsulated the whole sorry business came from one of Swans' official photographers, who said, 'There has been no political will to keep the yard alive . . . there is this misconception that shipbuilding is some sort of outdated, smoke-stack industry. But it isn't. Swans was at the forefront of technology. . .'

A reversal of fortune becomes less and less likely as the men with the skills have either left the area, retired or, in some cases, been gratefully re-employed by other industries.

It seems likely therefore that HMS *Richmond* will be the Tyne's last ship. When she left the river for delivery to the Royal Navy no more orders were outstanding and the berths and slipways stood quiet to await their final destiny.

It is now eight years since the first edition of this book and four since HMS *Richmond* was completed, and arguably the River has turned the corner from those long days of painful decline and has re-emerged with a brave and optimistic face, timed perfectly to coincide with Millennium money and a new acceptance by Tynesiders that no, the river will never be the same, and yes, the Tyne rebuild is into its next phase – let's say its fourth phase!

This acceptance has brought us to view sympathetically the post-industrial remains of a now distant time, and preservation of the Baltic Flour Mills is analogous with this spirit.

The past times were hard and very often cruel, but the views in this book show the magnificent achievements of military-like precision work that depended upon large-scale teamwork and demanded high prices from both workers and managers. We are still near enough in time to feel some of the pain of revisiting the demanding times as portrayed here, but we can now acknowledge that without that phase we would likewise not be where we are in time.

Other major changes since 1990 include even more expansion of off-shore construction work in and around the rotting stubs of former industries, but the exciting news announced as this book closed for press was a return to 'large' ship-repairing by the Tyne's A. & P. Appledore group, which clinched a £1.2 million contract for work on *Color Viking* against worldwide competition, including keen bids from Scandinavia and Northern Europe.

Other activities to be seen as the century closes include Scandinavian Seaways' *King of Scandinavia* regularly visiting North Shields from March 1998 on the service to Ijmuiden, and the ongoing conversion of dead and often contaminated tracts of land into pleasant riverside landscaped parks, walks and cycle ways, affording river devotees excellent views.

The biggest change must undoubtedly have been to the old Quayside at Newcastle. Gone are the last vestiges of trading days with the disappearance of crane and railway tracks and old warehouses near the river's edge (although some warehouses remain further back). The Ouseburn boat-owners club at the eastern end of the quay has been rehoused to the other side of the burn. The changes have also incorporated much of the Glasshouse Bridge/City Road area, with the re-profiling of roadways, etc. Arriving in the vacated spaces are hotels, wide promenade walks and crystal-palace 'speak-easies' lined by ornamental bollards. Behind this, city life is also affected, and the newfound buzz on the 'old' quayside is supplanting the older traditional meeting venues higher up in the old City – a challenge it must meet – as the change goes on.

A repeat of all this is found along the river-front at both North and South Shields. Anyone visiting the area after many years away would stare in disbelief, especially in the old dock area now occupied by the Royal Quays Shopping Malls!

I very much hope that younger generations of Tynesiders will take the trouble to find out about this unique and rich heritage into which they are lucky enough to have been born, and that the pictures will instil some curiosity and encourage some to visit the 'now' scenes of our 'past' pictures.

A stroll along the mellow Tyne in the autumn sun is a very good way to raise the industrial ghosts of the past. It is difficult to walk the new promenade along what was once Palmer's Empire and not perceive the powerful undertones of industrial might . . . the very river swell seems to whisper 'all that has gone before was done well'!

1. SCOTSWOOD TO REDHEUGH

Tell me grandad, tell me,
Of those days of Coaly Tyne,
When keelmen bustled up and doon,
And met the boats fra Lunnen Toon.

In 1620 this stretch of river was the most peaceful of settings, but almost imperceptibly the first river pollution showed itself in traces of coal dust that trickled into the main river bed from the mouth of the Team. The silt that formed the basis of a 350-year accumulation also ensured 15 generations of work for dredger crews and numerous other ancillary occupations.

By 1823 industry had seriously began to arrive and obliterate the rural setting and, after a further 70 years, the location was unrecognisable. Everywhere

lay soot below thick, rich smoke patterns. The river roads were in constant turmoil as ships of all shapes and sizes fought for their piece of territory off the new North Eastern Railway (NER) staith at Dunston and vied with the cruisers fitting out opposite at Elswick. The noise here was formidable: Elswick echoed to the barrage of Armstrong's workers beating iron plates and the constant crash of coal being teemed down Dunston's chutes.

Our maritime review begins above here, however, at Scotswood, where, within site of 'Dreadnoughts', children spent time wading with salmon nets and swimming when the weather suited. It is along this shore in the old parish of Whickham that industrial Tyneside started life, so it is an appropriate place to commence our journey. On the Whickham shore, or

---

Wherry

On the Tyne this word was used exclusively to describe the large clinker-built craft used for conveying raw and finished materials between yards/river sites, while also acting as lighters to ferry equipment/stores from visiting ships. They therefore developed to act as both lighters and barges. Originally propelled by oar and punt poles, convoys could easily be attached behind a steam tug to hitch a lift upstream. They became more and more self-powered via small steam donkey boilers, some even getting motor power just before their demise. Simple accommodation was afforded beneath one of the two end decks.

By 1900 there were 24 companies operating wherries, some wholly owned by the companies: the Tyne Wherry Co alone offered 24 craft ranging from 20 to 200 tons. Lightermen Allan Brown Ltd boasted almost 100, the largest fleet of steam wherries on the river, while some having small fleets were Cookson's Lead Works and United Alkali. The decline began after 1918 as fewer ships required bunkering or provisions brought alongside, but more detrimental was the advent of reliable road lorries who now did their work.

Wherry No 2 was employed by Vickers Elswick Works in carrying heavy machinery to downstream ships for export, etc. She continued work for Keedy & Sons in the 1950s carrying pre-fabricated steel sections to and from Hawthorn Leslie and other shipyard sites until made redundant in the early 1970s – one of the last then still employed.

Keel

These were used on the Tyne to convey a measurement of coal (about 21 tons) annexed to chaldron-size payloads. The name 'keel' was unique to the Tyne. Keels were mostly built using the carvel planking method (that is, giving the hull an all-over smooth finish, while the 'clinker' style produced a serrated profile).

Shell-clinker

A method of shipbuilding in which most of the hull is formed of overlapping planks with cross-wise frames added finally for strength. *Elswick No 2* was 55 feet long and 23 feet in the beam. She was constructed of 1-inch-thick oak planks nailed, in shell-clinker style, to closely spaced 5 inch by 6 inch frames. Strength was vital to withstand crushing when in heavy traffic.

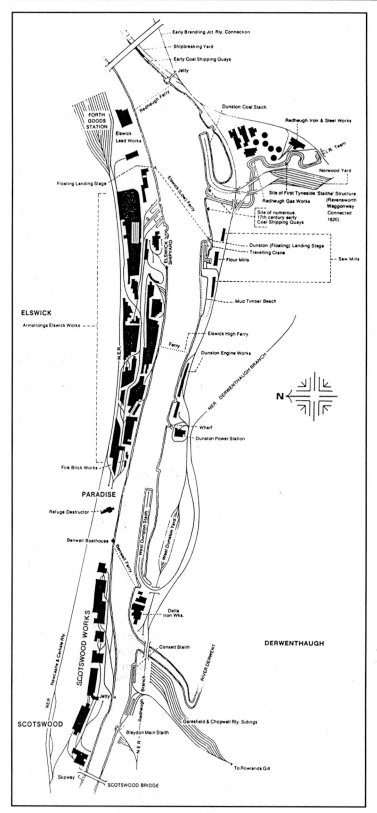

Left The Tyne: Scotswood to Redheugh

Above right In some places, where the tidal influence is much reduced, the Tyne was easily redirected and harnessed into almost canal-like servitude to facilitate the construction of large industrial sites upon particularly flat areas – at a premium on Tyneside. Here at Lemington in 1976, just off the west end of the map opposite, there are no signs of the once numerous old staiths, but many sidings for coal wagons for the two power stations at Stella have more than replaced them. Even these and the two fly-ash quays on the riverfront are now themselves but memories, as industrial evolution has moved another step forward in the race to produce cheaper power. The upper tidal limit, traditionally at Hedwin Sands, is not far from here. *UN*

Right In this second view we can see the Tyne snaking around the Newburn peninsula and skirting the Blaydon and Whickham fringes while collecting its first serious heavy industrial bi-products on the long journey to the sea. We are looking down the cooling towers of Stella North power station, now gone, while traces of smoke drift over the Tyne from the Stella South block. The quay for the ash-hoppers is clearly visible, as are the group of sidings at Newburn to accommodate the minerals for this coal-fired station. Both railway routes to the west can be seen on the extreme left and right of the picture. *UN*

Dunston riverfront, the salt marshes had become home for gas-works and coke ovens. Road and rail entwined at every corner and the river became suddenly claustrophobic as urban housing moved in ever closer and threatened to swamp that final small bit of greenery.

Just off the map on page 12 is Newburn, not only significant in transport history for the part it played in early railway developments, but also as the cemetery of the Tyne's last wherries, the successors of the keels. Deposited here by the Port Authority above the head of navigation after a river clean-up, they just missed preservation (see page 6), leaving the 1930s-built *Elswick No 2* as a last example of the old 'shell-clinker' style of construction.

Also within the 'S' shape described by the Tyne at Newburn and Lemington was 'power station land', which we briefly illustrate. Here the conical cones of the North and South Stella plants were a landmark until only a few years ago. These stations were served by steam-engine-hauled coal loads right up to the end of steam in this area in 1966. It was coal's bi-product, fly-ash, that brought the once familiar ash-hoppers, named after legendary local characters, on their frequent journeys up and down river to remove the ash to the sea dumping grounds.

Once on the map, on the south bank a short distance after Scotswood Bridge we encounter the first of the many staiths along this journey, Blaydon Main Staith. Alongside were Derwenthaugh Staiths, where the produce of the Consett-area pits materialised at river level, via the Garesfield & Chopwell sorting sidings. Today the remnant of the eastern-arm jetty is the base for a small marina.

Next comes the Derwent river-mouth and the location of Crowther's early iron works, as well as paper mills and fire-brick manufacturing, all using the raw power of tidal influence. Over the Derwent is the Delta Iron Works; dating from the late 18th century, it supplied Nelson's navy with grappling-irons and grape-shot to cannons. Next come the staiths at West Dunston, built just too late for the anticipated peak in coal demand and operated for a few years as an overflow to the main Dunston staith. Their associated wagon storage area is now the ballast underpinning the Metro Centre coach park.

Central to this area was Dunston Power Station. Built between 1931 and 1933, it was served by both wharf and rail connections until closure in

1981. Further, and about where was once an engine works, stood the famous scrapyard of Clayton & Davie (and finally run by T. J. Thompson). Many fine old vessels and steam engines were dismantled here. Housing and small industrial units have moved into this once dirty industrial area, while car-parking space for the Metro Centre dominates the remainder.

Past the site of Elswick High Ferry is the impressive Co-op Flour Mills that overlooked Elswick Works and were a first in this country in their scale of application of concrete and steel.

Dunston's now famously preserved staith is just beyond the Team mouth. At its height it saw 6 million tons of coal/coke shipped in one year, and survives today as a fascinating relic of a previous era in the Tyne's fortunes.

This area has a connection with 'coal-to-keel' that can be traced back to the very early 1600s and makes an interesting story as part of the evolution of industry.

At the southern limit of this area the central bridges area beckons, but before moving on let's quickly look at the northern bank.

From the Scotswood Bridge, which replaced the much-loved 1831 Chain Suspension Bridge in 1967, is an area dug deep in historic associations with Britain's once huge Empire. From here extended the 'Armstrong Corridor', perhaps the greatest ever Tyneside success story. Dating from 1847, Armstrong was forever expanding his manufacturing capabilities and developing ideas from his own scientific curiosity involving first hydraulics, then eventually armaments. Peripheral heavy engineering sprung up to give this area muscle only seen elsewhere at this time in Germany. Armstrong's Elswick Works became not only an employer second only to the shipyards on Tyneside, but also gave the area a new sense of pride, with its products seen worldwide; even today examples are in operation in many far corners of the world.

The Works will perhaps be best remembered for its 'Elswick Cruisers' launched before 1900, and the 'Dreadnoughts' soon afterwards. It became Armstrong-Mitchell's in the 1940s and later simply 'Vickers' before a slow demise in the 1970s resulted in the site's complete clearance in 1984, becoming today's promenaded 'walk of memories'.

Gateshead's late-lamented Jim Murray, once

shop steward convener at Vickers, maintained his 'cabin' at Elswick Works right up to the moment when the bulldozer arrived as the long, hard-fought campaign to save the Works finally failed. His own part in the attempt to save Vickers was imaginative and should still be remembered today by Tynesiders. On one occasion he went to Iran to see for himself the country that was for many years Vickers' main customer. He returned disgusted, saying, 'There are enormous social problems – 60 per cent infant mortality, throughout lack of good water – and here we are sending them tanks. It is a total waste of Tyneside's craftsmanship.'

Jim was typical of many bonny fighters from this region. He viewed his climb up the ladder of office with a mixture of cynicism and necessity. He was equally at home in his convener's cabin as in the Literary & Philosophical Society, and had either place sold Newcastle Scotch Ale he would never have needed to go elsewhere!

But life on the river wasn't exactly *all* heavy labour and confrontation, as this report confirms:

'The use of the river as a recreation resource should not be completely forgotten and the Tyne was the setting for many activities that drew spectators from all classes of society. The skiff race was staged from the Tyne bridge to Lemington and there was an annual

procession of barges on Ascension Day. An irregular regatta also coincided with horse races and other amusements going off in the area and led to the popularity of "gannin alang the Scotswood road" as an excellent vantage point. Harry Clasper was the most famous skiff oarsman on the Tyne.' (Buswell & Barke, *Newcastle's Changing Map*)

The lead in to the 'bridges' takes us past a conglomerate of gas, lead and glue works that created an ambience that is best forgotten. Needless to say railway connections were once everywhere, and the astute NER saw its chance here by buying-up Newcastle & Carlisle Railway property to develop into the Forth Goods Station. Nicely situated to the west of a city, then without traffic problems, the Forth acted as the main collection and delivery focal point until New Bridge Street depot was built in 1890. All now gone or going, the central cattle market office today forms the solitary centrepiece amid the soon to be opened Technology Park. It is the sole surviving piece of infrastructure from this once noisy part of Newcastle. Today's Arena complex sits upon a large part of the Forth Goods Station site, while rail maintenance equipment occupies the remaining bit of what once was a huge acreage of NER property.

In 1934 we are told in the Port of Tyne yearbook that '. . .the Consett Iron Co have recently erected two tanks for the storage of liquid tar and creosote near to their coal staiths at Derwenthaugh. . .' Here we see that those tanks have survived into the 1970s and have been joined by two others. We have caught a moment when this 'Consett staith' was still railed, although now severed from the hinterland. The Hurrocks allotment site is beyond Derwenthaugh sidings and this area is now swept over by the Western bypass – a continuation of the new road off Scotswood Bridge, seen here taking shape on the right and completed in the photograph overleaf. Over the Derwent Gut, Swalwell open-cast disposal concentration point is thriving and continued to do so until the miners' strike of 1983, when gradual run-down resulted in closure in the early 1990s. Local 'Metro' Radio is based alongside. *UN*

Above The starting point of 'Armstrong's Corridor' was where the Tyne is now crossed by the Scotswood Bridge, successor to the Chain Bridge. In the river in this circa 1970 view are the skeletal remains of the 'Consett staith' seen on the previous page, with the River Derwent flowing in behind. Flattened light-coloured areas appear where parts of the Elswick factories of an earlier time have been razed to break the continuity of this manufacturing strip alongside the Tyne. The hinterland housing still shows areas where Tyneside 'flats' in parallel rows exist. The shortage of trees has since been redressed amid the new topography that has come with the Newcastle Business Park. *UN*

Below This mid-point view of the 'Armstrong Corridor' along Scotswood Road was taken in the spring of 1983, at a time when the road itself formed a partition between the old way and the new. To the left is landscaping around green areas totally alien to the traditional Tyneside 'flats' culture of the early 20th century, where this would have been considered wasted house space for Armstrong's workers. The right-hand side, however, shows the still unbroken factory chain of Armstrong's World, his 'corridor of power', disappearing into the distance from a starting point well behind the camera. One of the many pubs, once located evenly along the 3-mile strip, can still be seen – now alone – as its time also runs out. The river glides silently past over massed roof vents. Today, re-profiled roads for the Newcastle Business Park have completely changed the character of this factory land. *KG*

Top A typical Elswick launch scene of the 1880s, when so many Elswick 'Cruisers' formed the backbone of the world's burgeoning 'modern' navies. They incorporated an evil-looking ram bow, the sort of thing that brought about the end of HMS *Victoria* in unfortunate circumstances when a manoeuvre went wrong. *SSL*

Middle and bottom Examples of two Tyne-built 'Dreadnoughts', both from Armstrong's Elswick 'war' Works and representing a most fascinating era in maritime building. The imagery of these awesome fighting machines still occupies the minds of many through some gripping plates of the day, as photography was also beginning to capture movement. These Battlecruisers could be described today as having a 'warts and all' honesty in their austerity, coupled with a kind of raw fearlessness that reflected Britain's rule of the waves and left an image that was frequently unshakable.

Armstrong's Battlecruiser HMS *Queen Mary* is seen off Tynemouth at a time when most of the world believed these ships to be invincible in battle. She was to prove lacking on 31 May 1916, when, in the first piece of action at the Battle of Jutland she was blown up with terrible loss of life. For the first time Britain realised that the German Navy had caught up!

The second example is the Elswick 'Cruiser' HMS *Superb*. She was launched in 1906, completed a year later, and is seen here off the mouth of the river on her trials. At this time the British Government vied for numerical supremacy with Germany, which brought about three orders for 'Dreadnoughts'; Armstrong-Whitworth won this one. Few will now remember the media slogan that ran 'We want eight [battleships] and we won't wait', as the competition between the countries hotted up. From 1908 turbine-fitted battleship orders were won as the approach to Jutland gained momentum. HMS *Superb* gained a battle honour at Jutland, and was the seventh RN ship to bear the name. She was scrapped by Stanlee in 1922. *Both SSL*

Harry Clasper

Born at Dunston in 1812, Harry Clasper went to work in the pits at Jarrow while still a child. After a time he got work as a cinder-burner at the Garesfield Coke Ovens and upon his 20th birthday got work as a wherryman for the same firm. Sculling boats at the time weren't over-graceful, and he began to design a vessel that would use streamlining to enable him to win in his sport of rowing. His perseverance of building his own vessel during the night – after work – paid off and he became Champion at the gala on the Tyne, commonly then known as Barge Thursday!

Prize money was relatively considerable then, with a win bringing £200, and when he also became Champion on the Thames he fame was assured. Goodness knows what he did with his money, but in 1861, at a testimonial for him, enough was raised to buy him a house in Scotswood Road, which he promptly turned into a pub. It was said at his testimonial: 'The London watermen laughed at you, Harry, when you brought down your new vessel design, but after [your victory] they quickly copied the design.'

Harry is unofficially credited with the shape of new sea-going clipper ships that appeared on the West Indies run soon afterwards. He died on 12 July 1870, aged 58 years.

Robert Chambers was one of Harry Clasper's conscripts to the art of sculling – and winning! 'Honest Bob' Chambers was born at St Anthony's in 1831 and spent his earlier years at Hawk's extensive iron works to work his way up to become a puddler. His strength was spotted by Clasper and he developed quickly under the latter's guidance to become the individual World Sculling Champion after having for six years held the Championship not only on the Tyne but also on the Thames. He died aged 37 years of consumption contracted as a reaction to over-training.

Above left A glimpse of the south bank of the Tyne looking over the Dunston, Teams, Lobley Hill and Whickham areas in a part of Gateshead that was at the forefront in the evolution of our home railways. The lie of the land is well illustrated as the coal measures in the green fields beyond in Northern Durham lie directly above the staith site at Dunston showing the bee-line preferred by early coal-owners to get their precious commodity to the river quickly. *UN*

Above The city end of the Armstrong factory chain is revealed in this early 1970 aerial view above Elswick and, to the right, Dunston waterfront, showing the whole of the staith. The Elswick and Scotswood Road high-rise flats that replaced the earlier cramped living conditions are themselves making way for low-rise construction, but fewer and fewer Geordies find employment along the riverbanks and it can be

seen that swathes of land have already been cleared to make way for the then planned riverside parks, walkways and business units. Inside the smoke-begrimed arc of the staiths at Dunston, the inner basin curve and its accompanying 'dolphins' (mooring buoys) are visible, while beyond is the soon to be cleared Redheugh Gas Works and the aromas connected therewith. In the right foreground can be seen the old ferry landing quay connected to the listed Co-op flour mills, already partly dismantled. Adjacent are the wood yards of Palmer Hall. Railways snake along both sides of the Tyne at this point. *UN*

Below A 1959 view of the 1891 Dunston CWS flour mills – the country's first on this scale constructed from ferro-concrete. The coaster *Moray Firth* is discharging at the suction hose, while two dumb concrete hopper barges stand by. *JJ*

Above A splendid example of commerce seen to be working in the raw elements of power generation in separate but interconnected forms is seen in this view across Redheugh Gas Works and Dunston Staith. It is about 1938 and there are few hints of the slips that once adorned the far shore of Elswick. Dunston Staith is operating at over 4 million tons of shipment a year and has the patiently awaiting colliers to prove optimum output. Redheugh Gas 'Factory' takes up a considerable acreage and is interwoven with railways that dart in and out from many sides, while its main supply source is seen coming into the view at the bottom right-hand corner. This is the Tanfield Railway and its connection into the Durham hinterland tapped a fine seam of gas and steam coal. At the top right-hand corner can be glimpsed the Redheugh drops adjacent to the Rabbit Banks. Of special interest in the evolution of staiths on Tyneside is the lowly River Team in its original course. It was just below the camera that a staith-like structure dating to circa 1620 has been identified as the earliest known hereabouts. *GL*

Above right A classic Tyneside river activity at Dunston Staith, once replicated in a hundred other locations throughout an industrial northern landscape. It is 1959, the inner basin staith is still in operation, and the Tyneside economy still relies upon Thames Gas, Light & Coke colliers

(the 'coal scuttle brigade'!) making the two-day journey up the coast.

A stalwart of the 1950s was Austin & Pickersgill (Wear) yard No 409, *Brunswick Wharf*. Completed in 1951 she joined the fleet of the British Electricity Authority, which in 1954 became the Central Electricity Authority. Her 'tidemark' illustrates her depth when loaded with 2,000 tons of northern coal. She ended her days after the decline of this business in 1974, and survived until quite recently as a cement storage hulk at Oslo, Norway. *JJ*

Right This is the outer staith, or river staith, at Dunston, the business end of a site that had seen coal trading, in various different forms, almost continuously from the 17th century. CEGB's *Sir Leonard Pearce* is receiving coal from spouts 3/4, while at 5/6 stands MV *Marius Nielsen*. The former was named after the Engineer-in-Chief of Battersea Power Station (knighted in 1935), and was constructed at Burntisland in 1941 for the then London Power Company. She was broken up on the Wear in the 1960s. *Marius Nielsen*, of 1954 vintage, was sold in 1970 to FOS Shipping and as the *Poliere* survived renaming only weeks, being wrecked at the Kettle Rock, off Tresco Island in the Scillies, while inward-bound from Foyness to Gdynia, Poland. *JJ*

Above This February 1979 view shows the junction of the Tanfield Railway and the Newcastle & Carlisle's Redheugh Branch at a point in the shadows of the now derelict Redheugh Gas Works. Storage gasometers, the black mass of Dunston Staith and derelict factories are not a place in which to find oneself at the dead of night! *KG*

Below We are now looking back towards the river and Dunston Staith over the massed ranks of Tyneside 'flats' above the Askew Road area of Gateshead circa 1956. It was such an outlook that gave rise to Gateshead being described by Priestly as 'the backlane to Newcastle', although the town has certainly shaken off that mantle today. This glimpse of the river really illustrates the point, however, showing the Tyne as nothing more than a black smudged industrial artery in its normal 1940s/1950s work-a-day garb. *GL*

Above This is Redheugh Quayside in 1895, looking up river towards the bridges of the day. This is the booming industrial Tyneside of the British Empire and world naval dominance, and is described enthusiastically by Johnson as teeming with activity and sound night and day. Although this was a quieter stretch, away from the noisy shipyard hammers, it can be seen that sideshow activity goes on everywhere.

No riverfront trading-space was ignored. To the right, a rail wagon pours, or 'teems', directly into the wherry *George Hope*, complete with collapsible sail; she is only a slight advancement upon her more famous predecessors, the keel boats. To wring every ounce from potential business, the NER has broken a few rules and positioned the rail on the very quay edge. Out in the river, steam paddle tug *William and Mary* leads another empty coal convoy up-river to other staiths. *Auty Collection, NCL*

Right In 1979 the Redheugh area shunt engine pays its final visit to the same location, which was then way beyond safe limits on an historic piece of metals. The area was visited twice daily until 1967, such was the activity of factories hereabouts. The hard-standing 'beach' for King's scrapping business below the old Redheugh Bridge is now empty. Industrial archaeology lies just below the surface at every turn. The line occupied by the 'pup' was once the Brandling Junction link line from Greenesfield down to the Newcastle & Carlisle branch. Out of view, hotels and promenade walks have now entirely replaced the timber storage yards along the far Newcastle bank. KG

2. THE BRIDGES TO ST PETER'S

Shipyard grease and shipyard oil,
Work, labour, sweat, toil,
Morn' till noon, noon till night,
Riveting, hammering with all oor might.

This stretch of river includes both Newcastle and Gateshead quaysides. The first bridge to span the Tyne ravine is said to have been the Roman bridge of 120 AD. It was possible – but only just – to negotiate the bridge by rowing boat at high tide. The second, medieval bridge of 1250 encouraged more movements below it, and consequently lasted until 1775, having seen hundreds of 'keels' come and go to the coal-rich banks upstream.

Today we have a bridge every few hundred yards, and the first encountered along our way is the new (1983) Redheugh Bridge. We next pass under the King Edward VII Bridge of 1906 (rail only) and almost immediately the Queen Elizabeth II (Metro) Bridge; again this is rail-only and used by the rapid transit 'trams'.

The remaining bridges, passed in quick succession, are the earlier group of High Level (1849), Swing (1876) and the Tyne Bridge (1928) itself. Started in 1925 the latter was a year *later* than the Sydney Harbour Bridge tender acceptance date, so to spoil the myth was *not* the model for the Australians to copy – a shame! It could be said that the bridges are the historical high-point, bearing in mind that each example celebrated new engineering techniques. The Swing Bridge is perhaps the most remarkable in its early application of the hydraulic concept. Its cost of construction was borne by river tolls that quickly paid off the debt after 1893, with the constant comings and goings to the busy (and then new) staiths at Dunston. It was required to 'turn' almost hourly, night and day, before the 1960s and was a great sideshow attraction to dads and children! At its busiest in about 1924 6,000 ships with a net payload tonnage of 6,327,847 passed each

way. Today, with a revived interest in the Tyne, demonstration 'swings' are possible.

Moving on to the quayside area, we come to the traditional heartland of trading. Excavations by the University have recently revealed that early shipbuilding went on here, at the original shoreline perhaps 50 metres back from the current quay-edge. Much important maritime heritage left for the future is to be found at the Trinity House Museum, the traditional home of the Master Mariners of Newcastle. Its roots go back to the year of incorporation as a Guild in 1505, when its responsibilities covered lighthouses, buoys and (the eventual source of much complaint) control and regulation of the hundreds of river and sea pilots. The implementation of a separate 'Tyne Pilotage Board' in 1865 gave the service a dedicated administrative body that today handles the business of the remaining half-dozen river-pilots and their two operational boats. Trinity House is open to the public and is a 'must' for shipping enthusiasts, as is the excellent collection in the maritime section of the Discovery Museum in Blandford Street, Newcastle (formerly called the Museum of Science and Engineering).

Over the years the quayside has played host to many different types of vessels at its 26 berths. A common Corporation landing stage nearby is still in use today as the embarkation point for gentle river trips. Along the Quayside were, until quite recently, berths dedicated to the various trading companies, such as the Tyne-Tees Shipping Company, which also had a considerable area across at Hillgate Quay, Gateshead. Further around the curve, beyond the Ouseburn mouth, was the regular berthing location for the Scandinavian 'butter-boats' and mainly Danish boats, filled with butter-barrels. The curved wood of the disposed barrels was once a familiar sight around Tyneside, as it was a great source of extra earnings for small boys as firewood.

The Tyne was generally dredged to a depth of 30 feet below low water (ordinary tides), and at the end of the 1930s the total quay area extended to 2,000 feet. In 1934 the river boasted an incredible 60 regular weekly foreign 'steamship' services. We haven't the space to list them all, but each Saturday there was a sailing to Antwerp with the Tyne-Tees Steamship Company. Also on Saturdays (during the summer months) you could leave for Arendal aboard the ships of the Det Bergenske Dampskibsselskab. Bordeaux was serviced once weekly by the General Steam Navigation Company, while Corunna (as traffic demanded) was served by MacAndrew Line vessels. Surprisingly, Istanbul was connected by three operators, giving a roughly fortnightly service from Newcastle Quay! One went via Bremen, another via Hull, and one direct by way of the Westcott & Laurance Line Ltd. It seems difficult to believe today, but Newcastle Quay had more destinations than today's airport!

To the east end of Hillgate Quay, on the Gateshead side, is the shore-based RNVR HMS *Calliope*. The first drill ship used was an old corvette dating from 1885; she went to the shipbreakers in 1951, replaced by the sloop *Falmouth*, renamed *Calliope*. (The photograph on page 30 shows her fate.)

The fringe of this section of the river takes us up to St Peter's and includes the Ouseburn/Glasshouse area. From *Newcastle's Changing Map* (Buswell & Barke) we are given a clue about the Tyne's glass connection:

'Around 1860 Sir Robert Mansell, prompted by laws forbidding the use of

The heart of the region is clearly illustrated in this view taken in 1976. The nearest bridge, the old Redheugh, was originally designed by Thomas Bouch and built in 1870, but was rebuilt six years later following lessons learned from the Tay Bridge disaster. It has since been replaced by its 1983 successor. Next, the King Edward Bridge brings the main East Coast railway across the void. Missing is the Metro Bridge, opened by Her Majesty Queen Elizabeth II in 1981.

The 'city' group follows, crossing at the traditionally narrowest point. First is the High Level Bridge, designed by George Stephenson's son Robert and built by 1849, the original main-line route for Anglo Scottish trains but now carrying lighter traffic while still used by road vehicles at a lower level. The Swing Bridge was built in 1876 by William Armstrong, and finally the 'logo' of the region, the Tyne Bridge of 1928, completes the six bridges that span the Tyne gorge within 500 yards. *UN*

timber in glass making, took out a patent and set up a glasshouse at the mouth of the Ouseburn using the readily available cheap coal from Heaton and Byker and locally abundant ballast sands and cheap ballast cargo in returning coal ships. This site was near enough to Newcastle to take advantage of the town's loading facilities but far away enough not to be a nuisance. The later glasshouses situated in Closegate and Skinnerburn districts had the advantage of cheap coal from Elswick but had the additional costs in having to use keels up beyond the bridge. Further upstream, Lemington glasshouses, which

had started in 1760, produced glass until the mid-1930s.'

Slightly further eastward, the early Marble Works shown on the map was replaced in 1949 by the impressive Baltic Flour Mills. Today the mill is empty and the adjacent animal food factory demolished, leaving a huge silo as a reminder of the days when 20,000-ton merchantmen would tie up alongside; as mentioned elsewhere, the site is to become a visual arts display centre by the year 2000. There is so much of maritime interest in this half-mile from Redheugh through to Sandgate, but it only now remains for us to arouse your curiosity more by means of the pictures.

Left   The Tyne: the Bridges to St Peters

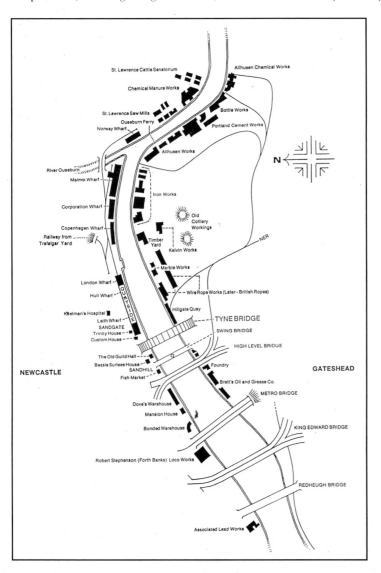

Above right   From this aerial view above Dunston Staiths can be seen the Tyne as it begins to describe a large figure 'S'. Prominent in this view of a still 'five-bridged' Tyneside of the 1960s are the heavy railwayed installations at the Forth area on the left. From here there were connections into gas works, lead works, tanneries and Armstrong's Works. Partially seen at the extreme left is the Central Station, and across the river is Pipewellgate, which once supported the mass of the Greenesfield Engine Works and sheds of the NER. Both the large flour mills – Baltic and Spillers – can be seen in this view, with miscellaneous shipping strung out in between. *UN*

Right   Swinging to the south, this is the view in 1969 from above Gateshead looking at the heartland of the City, or 'toon' as it is known locally! Among the bridges the minesweeper used in a fisheries protection role is lying adjacent to the Guildhall, but other quays are devoid of activity. A look over the City area reveals the split then apparent between the older, blackened properties – many since demolished – and the newer buildings, exemplified by Swan House above the Tyne Bridge, which from this height appears to be unsupported. *UN*

Above These four photographs take us on a nostalgic river trip downstream through the heart of the regional capital on fly-ash hopper *Bessie Surtees* in 1958. Owned by the Central Electricity Generating Board, London, she was completed by Charles Hill & Sons of Bristol in 1955. She was a regular feature of the river shuttling to and from the power stations at Dunston and Blaydon until her disappearance in the 1980s.

The first view can be compared with the 1895 scene on page 23. The old Redheugh Bridge is looking jaded, and on the right, where we saw sailing wherries loading coal in 1895, there are the remnants of three of what are thought to be Castle Class corvettes. This class was constructed late in the Second World War and saw out the final days supporting our tired convoys. Much of their building programme was abandoned. Over on the Newcastle side to the left, little appears to have altered since 1895 and timber sheds litter the foreshore together with the first of the many abandoned wherries. *JR*

Below We are now nearing the King Edward Bridge, with, on the right, the corvette HMS *Alnwick Castle* in her last resting place below the banks of Pipewellgate, Gateshead. Greenesfield Engine Works with its many chimneys is silhouetted above. Midway over the bridge, a Class 'J39'

steam locomotive stands near the cut-out metal 'county' name signs. *Bessie Surtees*'s foremast can be seen in the collapsed position in preparation for the lower bridges. The ship's bell is also in good view. *JR*

Above The City group of bridges beckons *Bessie* onward and we see the daunting prospect of the Swing Bridge clearance height in the normal – closed to river traffic – position. Brett's Oil & Grease building is on our right, and high above it Gateshead East station, still fully roofed, commands an excellent view to the north. *JR*

Below We are now looking east, showing the up-stream approach to the City area. From this outlook the Tyne Bridge, still today the region's icon, makes a commanding sight to those visiting for the first time. The Quayside warehouse sheds and cranes on the right are quiet upon this occasion, while on our port side we are about to pass Japanese motor vessel *Seikai Maru* of 1954, unloading flour at the Baltic Flour Mills. A pedestrian 'tippler' bridge of a unique design is intended to span the river at this point as part of a £33 million expenditure to revive and convert the now defunct Mills into an Arts Centre easily accessed from the Newcastle side. *JR*

Above left With a backcloth of Redheugh station, the Rabbit Banks and the serried rows of house-ends of Gateshead's Bensham district, *Hexhamshire Lass* sallies forth on her preferred safe mid-stream approach to the upper reaches of the river en route to the Stellas and another fly-ash load in 1959. *JJ*

Left In the shadow of the Tyne Bridge, and beyond it the High Level Bridge, Sylvia Steel, one of the WRNS permanent staff at the RNR shore establishment at Gateshead, watches her former training ship, HMS *Calliope*, being towed away to the breakers yard of Hughes Bolckows at Blyth on a grey 30 April 1968. *SSG*

Above The Swing Bridge is fully open to allow the collier *Minster* to make the final leg of the long journey from the Thames to the staiths at Dunston, glimpsed straight ahead. Her tallest mast has just cleared the High Level Bridge at river flood and she is carefully observed by dads and children not very far above. In 1847 many thought Stephenson's monumental early work impossible to achieve but he didn't just achieve the impossible – it remains today in active service albeit slightly tight for passing buses on the lower road deck. The riverfront buildings seen beyond have since been swept away completely and the site occupied by the 1994 Copthorne Hotel. Skirting past the hotel and all along the riverfront is a pleasant promenade walk that could never have been even remotely imagined at the time of this scene, with the scattering of small disjointed businesses and buildings, many in poor condition. Time was, before the Metro Centre, large cinema complexes and high car ownership, that a good day out involved a stroll along the river with an hour on a bridge watching the traffic or other people working, then home to tea. How our habits have changed since 1960! The weather certainly seems to have improved. *JJ*

Above A typical day's activity along Newcastle's riverfront in early 1960, as the tug *Maximus* brings up TIC Dredger No 8. On the Quayside, Commer and Bedford lorries wait their turn to back on to the conveyor belt hopper feeding aggregates into the hold of the coaster *Queensgate*. Victualling and de-spoiling goes on around the hull of the vessel that dwarfs the buildings of the Quayside. The photograph was taken from the Control Office of the Swing Bridge in its open-to-river-traffic position. *JJ*

Below A nice wide sweeping view of Newcastle Quayside occupied by large and small vessels in April 1960. *JJ*

Above right The photographer has had it in mind to capture the bustle of the Sunday morning market from the Tyne Bridge, and in doing so has captured a quayside roof-top view of considerable antiquity now that so much has altered. The coaster *Rocket* is adjacent to a large mobile crane, and a yellow and white Corporation bus on route 29 attempts to ease through the throng. *KG collection*

Right In the 1970s the devaluation of the pound encouraged a Scandinavian invasion, especially prior to Christmas! This scene, in November 1975, although at a time of North Sea storms, coincided with crews eager to participate in a shopping expedition along Newcastle's well-known Northumberland Street. This is perhaps the nearest the Quayside came to echoing the busy days when a forest of masts was a common sight. *SSG*

Left The foreground small timber ranch-style shed hardly compares with the new large warehouses further back along the Quayside. Two massive river hoists connect directly into the goods shed, revealing a high degree of automation for the early 1900s. The other details repay careful investigation, as they say so much about Tyne life at this time, from the grindstone wheels to the various trolleys and the timber structure for conveyance to vessels or road transport. *NCL*

Below left The view in the opposite direction some 70 years later allows us a spot of 'time travel' to see the final industrial format of sheds and roadways lying behind the more familiar riverfront views seen elsewhere within. We can see that all sheds are of a standard height and width in their final form, with the railways to facilitate commerce equally complete with rails snaking in all directions and as far as Glasshouse Bridge seen in the left distance. Timber loads, no doubt from a Scandinavian coaster, await their respective tractor units on this quiet March morning in 1969. On the extreme left the railway leaves through a tunnel, concealed in the shadowed area. The white building on the right skyline is Spillers flour mill, still extant. It was built in 1936, then Europe's largest flour mill, capable of handling 250,000 tons of grain. The firm's products are still well known and include a sizable range of canine appetisers! *KG*

Above right An earlier view of the tunnel that led the railway from the Newcastle Quayside up to storage and distribution to the City from the New Bridge Street Goods Depot. The tunnel mouth was one of the last of the old Quayside features to disappear, in 1997, shortly before production of this book. *J. W. Armstrong Trust*

Right The view from above the tunnel mouth in September 1969, after rail use had finished here in June of that year. Compared with the upper view opposite, no trace remains of the hoist connection into the shadowed warehouse, its day almost done. Sadly, there is little evidence of this heritage portrayed to today's visitors to the City, except in books such as this. *KG*

Above left Mid-way along the new quay extension to the east of the City, tramp trader *Crusader*'s winches and donkey engines are framed in the legs of a crane while loading bags of anhydrite originating in Cumbria. *JJ*

Left The Baltic Flour Mills forms a striking backdrop to this busy river scene taken in April 1961. In central river is *Bessie Surtees* again, named after the heroine of Sandgate, a mere 100 yards away. At the Quayside is the coaster *Chevychase* – another name steeped in northern folklore – with the tug *Eastsider* paying her close attention, while over the river at the big mill is *Leeds City* (a 1955 product of the neighbouring Wear for Rearden Smith and registered at Bideford) discharging flour.

The Baltic mill has been the centre of some controversy lately. Once expected to be demolished along with all the other defunct dockside artifacts that lay opposite, it survived just long enough to prosper with one of the biggest Millennium lottery grants ever bestowed upon the North East. £33 million will be spent on turning the old mills into a arts centre specialising in audio-visual displays. A pedestrian bridge will cross the gap from Newcastle Quayside, its 'butterfly wing' structure designed to open to allow tall masts beneath. These additions to the quay scene will no doubt help to attract peripheral occupations, not to mention visitors to the old spiritual centre of the region. Tyneside holds its breath. . . *JJ*

Above A closer view of the massive Baltic Flour Mills, which dwarfs *Leeds City* lying alongside emptying. *JJ*

Above left A recently acquired war prize, the *Empire Conifer* slips downstream through a still war-weary and grey-coated Quayside in 1946. She started life at Emden in 1935 as the *Adrian*, but was ceded to Britain after the war and came briefly under the management of Tyne-Tees Shipping. She was resold in 1947 to Australian interests.

Here she is coming under the eagle eye of some local boys – perhaps dreaming of visiting those faraway places that the ship touched. *UN*

Left Beyond the old Quayside area east of the City was a natural division where the Ouseburn stream ran into the Tyne. Developed with Tyne Improvement Commission works early in the century, this area came to be known for its high preponderance of 'butter boats', visiting vessels and their Scandinavian produce. This 1962 view evokes memories of a time when a small army would descend upon the quay early each morning for the chance of some work. *Olivian Coast* and *Frisian Coast* are at the butter-quay, while beyond is the *Exedene*. *JJ*

Above Netherlands Coast lies alongside the splendidly white concrete mass of a still recent Spillers Flour Mill above its new quay extension in 1960. Fly-ash hopper *Bessie Surtees* (again!) plods by at her customary 10 knots en route to her North Sea dumping ground. *JJ*

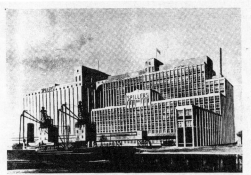

The high plated walls of *Cairnavon* form a formidable barrier in this view at Spillers Quay in 1958. *Cairnavon* was built as the *Empire Snow* in 1941 for the Government's war effort by Charles Connell on the Clyde. She had a counter-stern design with a gross tonnage of 6,372. Bought by Cairns Noble of Newcastle in 1946, she was renamed and eventually went for scrap in 1968, then under Lebanese ownership. Cairns Noble were at this time the Tyne's only deep-sea liner company and specialised in Canadian traffic from East Coast ports. Their company symbol, seen upon the funnel, represents a Scottish cairn – a pile of stones in a conical shape. *JJ*

INTERLUDE:
RIVER PEOPLE

Johnny Landers, one of Dunston Staith's 'characters', takes a breather from the hot work of 'teeming'. His clogs and protective equipment were supplied by the BR Staff Clerk Mrs Brenda Crosby down at the Yard Master's Office at Dunston, who also had the unenviable task of keeping their pay correct. Customised wagon brakes lie around with some home-made devices to make the job easier. *KG*

The export process at the business end may not have been pretty but it was very functional. The distinctly Victorian lines of the staith structure at Dunston challenge the sleek 1970s sheer of MV *Bongo*. The space left aft is in case there is need for ballasting. *KG*

Above While the 'teemers' up above had the job of making the mineral run, those responsible for the trim, and thus the safety of the vessel to achieve its destination upright were the 'trimmers'. They were, as far as I know, always employed by the Port of Tyne Authority, and their pay was slightly easier to calculate! MV *Bongo* completes her payload and soon the crew will miraculously appear only minutes before time to weigh anchor after giving their legs a stretch with landlubbers. *KG*

Left A commodity that required many hands during transshipment was timber, most frequently landed at Albert Edward Dock, although for other than pit-props Tyne Dock was the more suitable handling location. The latter, with its neighbouring timber-seasoning yard at Jarrow and a vast storage acreage, fed yards such as Pyman Bell's, with its own internal railway system. The many thousands of tons of timber imported in all shapes and sizes brought about an unspoken order to events, and an unpublicised language in communications between handlers and crane operators ensured that incidents were few. *Tacoma Star*'s donkey winches are in action. *JJ*

Above If timber required to be seasoned it would be dropped overboard into the river. This is a simplistic description of what was quite complex work, again requiring many years of work on the river. The planks needed to be tethered in the correct proportions to ensure that they would remain under control if a strong swell was running in the main river. These timber rafts could be four or five layers deep, and as many as 200 planks could be transported in one lift to the mud flats of Jarrow Slake. They would remain afloat there sometimes for many years depending upon demand and their building purpose. *JJ*

Right Scandinavian coasters frequently arrived with timber requiring transshipment to smaller craft, such as this barge standing in the vicinity of Tyne Dock Engineering's yard near South Shields. The river's lightermen undertook a diverse range of duties and responsibilities. *JJ*

Left Taken in the railway-built-and-owned Tyne Dock during the 1940s, this British Council wartime publicity picture is simply entitled 'Unloading wheat in Tyne Dock'. It does nevertheless further demonstrate the diverse commodities once dealt with by the many hundreds of lighters and barges seen on countless rivers all around the British Isles at that time. The advent of containerisation in the 1960s changed all this for ever and brought an end to manual work for many hundreds of foyboatmen on large-scale importing rivers such as the Tyne then was. *UN*

Left The once traditional dockers' role of portage and crane-liaison work is seen again here in this view of jute bales being off-loaded into the Quayside warehouses with their huge sliding doors and concrete post buffers – now gone. *JJ*

Right Leaving the Tyne this time are bags of ammonia from the Warrington area that have arrived at Tyne Dock after a 300-mile round rail trip in their LMS wagons. The high bridge of the cargo steamer oversees operations in this 1947 picture. *UN*

Left Another British Council publicity picture, this one showing one of Cochrane's large condensing boilers being safely stowed aboard a ship in Tyne Dock. This vessel appears to have had a concrete hold cover made (bomb-proofing?). Some excellent steamer deck detail is on show, while the children indicate that this is certainly after the war years and also maybe summertime. *UN*

Below left Some dockside export work was done under the eagle eyes of a passenger ship's experts! Here MV *Braemar* at Commissioners Quay makes ready for the journey to Bergen/Oslo. Including the crane operator (seen for once) there are 13 men overseeing this lift operation, but the end of the era of 'many hands' is fast approaching evidenced by the Reefer Container already stowed away on deck. Passenger were well entertained before departure in those days! *JJ*

Above right Not only are there lightermen and foyboatmen employed in the lesser but important role of marshalling and mooring these huge metal tugs, but there were also those involved in pilotage, fire-fighting craft, maintaining the lights and fog signalling equipment, and floating crane operations that rarely got a mention. Today the remaining equipment is automated. *Welsh Trader* (of 1954, belonging to the Trading Navigation Co of London) is seen at Sutherland Quay while

its imports are being pushed around by cranemen and lightermen into the barges below for onward distribution. *JJ*

Below Not so obviously visible to the many folk who couldn't resist trawler-watching at North Shields fish quay were the hundreds of tidying, repairing and maintaining duties that are an endless daily slog for those that go to sea in small boats. This late 1950s view shows trawlermen at work and illustrates just how quickly trawler designs have moved on, now even requiring an understanding of high-tech electronic aids and associated equipment. There is little 'wooden' about today's fleet – although the chores aren't so very different! *JJ*

Below Blacksmiths are repairing ships' anchor cables in an empty South Shields shipyard dry dock. That six men were involved in what may be seen to us today to be a trivial task demonstrates not only the thoroughness of all operations then, which had a safety implication, but also the many learning levels evident, involving specialist tools and techniques. *SSG*

Bottom More advanced metalwork is demonstrated by this view inside Parsons Marine Engineering works at Heaton in December 1958, which has to be included if for no other reason than to allow us to boast of the superb precision tooling machinery that contributed to countless millions of trouble-free miles sailed by the thousands of vessels fitted with Parsons engines. The firm's biggest claim to fame has to be the development of the steam turbine by the founder, Sir Charles Parsons. It not only revolutionised maritime trading speed and reliability worldwide but put Great Britain into a class of her own to continue dominating the shipping lanes of the world for a further 50 years. *NCL*

Above right Dirty, ugly dredgers were never in the limelight, but made it possible for us to have the drama and the majesty of a launch, and at such times were even more likely to have crept back into their black holes under cover of darkness somewhere along the riverbank. Even more mysterious were the men who manned these contraptions! Occasionally dredgers were seen in full public view in daylight, and came as a shock to those unsuspectingly stumbling upon them, who were surprised that such things could float, looking more like some sixth-form experiment gone wrong!

One dredger that did appear in the sunlight was Tyne Improvement Commissioners No 8, seen earlier on page 32. In the full glare of Newcastle Quayside she is being towed upstream towards Dunston on a March day in 1960. The men at her bow were employed in dirty and often dangerous work; just one of the hazards in this part of the world were wartime mines, which pop up in odd places even today. *JJ*

Right Another very necessary job on the river that was seldom witnessed and even less understood was the work of the river police. Hazardous and often quite gruesome work fell to these men, who traditionally had little protection in a launch of the scale of No 8 seen here. *JJ*

Left It was particularly difficult to find an image to do justice to the skilful, highly exacting and very necessary work of the Tyne pilots – especially an image showing their work in action. I had despaired of finding anything appropriate when a friend of Thomas Purvis (a pilot on the river today) kindly offered this view. My search was over!

Thomas explained that this was a picture of his father, and pointed out that the uniform included a distinctive cap and heavy stormcoat, all of which had to be hauled up steel walls such as this on perhaps a dozen or more occasions each day in the busy times up to the 1970s. The technique being adopting here is to pull a side of the ladder off the steel to make a foothold easier, all part of the skills of self-survival. To attempt this in gales off the Tyne, when the pilot boat was crashing about threatening to crush you against the vessel, demanded a certain coolness, not to mention agility! *Courtesy of Mr T. H. Purvis*

Above right Although not following a maritime occupation, the men that 'crewed' these riverside shanty towns have a right to be included as 'river people'. The reason why so many riverside peripheral strips were made over to pigeon lofts and allotments could well have been something to do with the smells and the ambient temperatures that went with them! It must be explained that a riverside flat with a mooring wasn't always so eagerly sought. Examples still exist, especially at Walker; these were found above Gateshead South Shore Road in 1964, not far from the Baltic Flour Mills. Over the river is the Glasshouse Bridge area and a lone deep-sea trawler. *KG*

Right People on the Tyne were also not just restricted to river workers! Although hardly leisure cruise conditions prevailed in the mid-1950s, there were many fascinating sites even on a Shields river crossing, including a small detour amongst the moored vessels awaiting attention for various different reasons. This party of schoolchildren seems to have caught the eye of some 'wags' intent on some fun, much to the girls' amusement. I think we can assume the nature of the dialogue! This picture is the sort that demands the 'whatever became of them, what was their fate, where are they now?' sort of questions! *SSG*

'When I was a boy I spent my time
Sitting on the banks of the River Tyne,
Watching all the ships going down the line
. . . they were leaving. . .'
(With acknowledgments to Roger Whittaker and his song
'Durham Town'.) *KG*

Just watching the ships. . . Mother and child, South Shields,
16 September 1960. *SSG*

3. ST PETER'S TO LOW WALKER

*My Fatha was born at Dent's Hole, my Motha
was born in Losh, Wilson & Bell's factory
cottages – Walker-on-Tyne. Her Fatha's brother
was the foreman-cooper at Locke Blackett's Lead
Works. The wife's grandfatha was a tugboat
owner on the Tyne.*

(From Pottery Bank People)

In 1880 local historian R. J. Charleton said of
this location below Byker:

'That part of Riverside Newcastle . . . smoke-
blackened and neglected as it is . . . presents a
rare field to those who delight in the old-
fashioned and the picturesque. To the casual
visitor who crosses the Glasshouse Bridge the
place, after the bustle and stir of the Quayside,
appears to sleep a heavy and bedrugged sleep,
disturbed now and then by the uneasy dreams
of work; for whatever work goes on here is
shut in by walls and palings, and gives no
outer sign except it to be in the shape of
additions to the already dense enough cloud
of smoke which hangs overhead. . .'

The St Peter's Works of R. & W. Hawthorn would
have certainly figured in this overview, and the
report may have reflected the transshipments of
machinery from Hawthorn's Forth Banks Works
(close to Stephenson's Locomotive Works, in
South Street) to here, which had become necessary
owing to a slump in locomotive orders and an 1880s
boom in marine engine orders. This riverfront site
gave Hawthorn's their opportunity to diversify, and
soon the company's Works at St Peter's was
working hand-in-glove with Charles Mitchell,
supplying the majority of his ships with machinery.

In 1883, in view of increasing technological
complexity, the North East Coast Institution of
Engineers & Shipbuilders was founded and the
Chief Mechanical Engineer of Hawthorn's, F. C.
Marshall, played a large part in encouraging its
growth. The following year, the two Hawthorn sites
were managed separately. For many years,
Marshall's excellent marine engines were second to
none, as indicated by a well-filled order book;
however, with the development of Parson's turbine,
the name of Marshall was to become forgotten.

The advent of the iron ship meant that bigger
shipyards were needed and many small family
shipyards, such as Gaddy & Lamb, were to
disappear, for beyond the 1860s building with iron
became essential to survival.

We will hear more about Andrew Leslie in the
next chapter, but suffice to say here that an
amalgamation of two companies with a fine
maritime record in 1886 brought about the
formation of Hawthorn Leslie, a name eventually
known throughout the world. The St. Peter's
Works continued to produce marine engines,
while over the river Fair's small yard had become
the expanding shipyard of Mitchisons (1919).
Tugs, trawlers and smaller craft emanated from
here, and in 1964 the Friars Goose Marina
Management Group took over the slip.

Further down river, past St Anthony's Point, we
eventually come to the former site of Marconi
Radar. At about this location was the well-known
Wood Skinner's yard. Operating by 1883, many
fine steam 'tramps' and colliers were constructed
here, but fierce competition had by 1924 driven
orders elsewhere. Around Bill Point, the recently
operating Harrison's slipway brings us into a
straight stretch of river renowned the world over
for its heavy shipbuilding industries. The north
bank was covered by iron works, graving docks,
slips or huge stock-piling sheds. The south bank
was, in contrast, the scene of frenzied coal teeming
at a point at the end of many lines connecting to
the vast North Durham pit railway complex.
These staiths had their own 'pub' amidst the

mound of settled coal-dust: Moloney's Bar was an interesting industrial feature named after an Irish character. Getting thrown out of here invariably meant an early shower – in the Tyne!

The next shipyard along, owned by J. D. Morris, built next to an early defunct coal-spout, came and went within six years. As we approach Hebburn (and the next stretch of the river) note the crossing place, until quite recently one of the Mid-Tyne Ferry landings. A photograph of one of their functional vessels can be found in the next chapter. A history of the Tyne's ferry services would make interesting reading, but unfortunately such a book awaits publication.

Again much preceded the established maritime trades hereabouts, and this synopsis from *Newcastle's Changing Map* perhaps says everything:

'One impetus to the development of the chemical industry in the area can be dated to 1778 when Losh, having developed a process using untaxed spoilt salt from the spring at King Pit in Walker and cheap coal locally, opened an alkali plant at Low Walker. Chemical factories and plants again developed along the Tyne and concentrated in Walker, Ouseburn, Skinnerburn and Bell's Close. With something like 300,000 to 400,000 tons of alkali waste being produced on the Tyne each year and smoke and poisonous gases being expelled, there were several complaints. Alderman Donkin lodged complaints against the many alkali factories in the Byker and Walker areas.

By the 1890s the industry was in a serious decline and by early in the 20th century had largely left the inner-city area, leaving

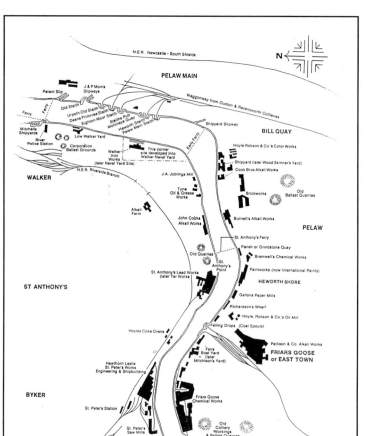

Left The Tyne: St Peter's to Low Walker

Right A seldom recorded activity that local people were almost apologetic about were the shipyard workers' trains that ran on an electric loop off the coast circular route. This deviation threaded together the unlikely stations of Point Pleasant and Carville while running during peak hours only to facilitate the uplift of shipyard workers from these stations together with Willington Quay and Walker. In this 1969 view, where the line momentarily tottered upon the edge of the river above Byker Sands, the electric service has given way to diesel trains, and this unit is leaving St Peter's after dropping off any Hawthorn Leslie workers. Opposite, in a freezing mist, is Friars Goose Marina and the river's designated main swinging area, for the reversing of all but the biggest vessels – hence the wide sweep of water. *KG*

behind only the paint manufacturing and pharmaceutical industries.

Soap manufacturing was well advanced before 1800 and used animal fats from the meat and tanning trades as well as waste from the glass and later chemical factories. Many lessees began to forbid the production of objectionable smells and in 1829 the Corporation of Newcastle sued Doubleday & Easterly for causing a nuisance with their soapworks in the Close.'

Finally, we take a last look along the north bank; note the remains of the 'Naval' yard opened in 1912 by Armstrong-Whitworth to relieve its Elswick Yard. Many fine battleships including HMS *Queen Mary*, HMS *Malaya*, HMS *Nelson*, HMS *Agincourt* and HMS *King George V* were built here, together with aircraft carriers. Closed in 1928, reopened and closed again in 1931, then finally again in the mid-1970s, the yard had a somewhat chequered existence. The 1930s mini-revival was solely due to

Vickers transferring the building of the liner *Monarch of Bermuda* from the company's Barrow Yard. After the next naval boom-time for the Second World War, the yard settled down into building several passenger ships of high quality. In the mid-1950s, the same yard constructed many high-quality freighters for locally managed shipping companies, and eventually saw out its days finishing other yards' products.

Charles Mitchell's yard, founded in 1853, was adjacent to the ferry. As early as 1867 Mitchell's warships were armed by Armstrong, but in spite of this close working relationship amalgamation didn't follow until 1882. The firm later became Armstrong-Whitworth and eventually Vickers.

In 1934 there were just seven shipbuilding yards remaining operational on the river with a total of 54 slips. The depressed conditions had closed 42 building slips – almost half of the Tyne's building/repairing capacity had gone with thousands of jobs within four years. The river was never to be quite the same place again!

Left The old Hoyles Coke Ovens (now allotment gardens) provide an interesting viewpoint across the Tyne, including Hawthorn Leslie's cranes against the backdrop of the Tyne Bridge beyond the river's description of a huge letter 'S'. The 1954-built *Vaigu* skirts St Peter's and Byker 'sands' with a coke load from Dunston Staith in September 1973. Hardly designed for collier work, some improvisation is evident with the addition of 'greedy boards' to maximise the payload and extend her life a little further. She represents a type of general ocean tramp trader that once numbered many thousand, many from North East yards. *KG*

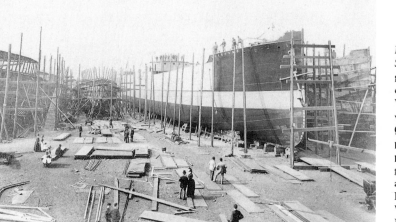

Left The launch of the Steamer *Skarpsno* in 1889 is witnessed by guests that may include the wives and children of the row of senior officials of Wood Skinner's Yard. Over 300 vessels were launched from these Bill Quay slips between 1883 and 1925. A post and derrick system using horse-power was employed for lifting from ground level the large plates seen lying about. This site was originally an old Bottle Works alongside the early Washington Staith. *National Maritime Museum*

The bend in the river at Bill Point was, until 1880, almost unnavigable to large vessels due to the cliff outcrop here. Compare this view with the map on page 54 and you will notice that the Tyne Oil & Grease Works location is now, by 1976, a dark smudge of contaminated land and in its dying days, whereas the Jobling's Mill site has been cleared and partially occupied by the expanded Naval Yard. The fitting-out quay is located near sheds that were once part of Losh, Wilson & Bell's iron foundry. Across the river are landscaped walkways and cycleways where once a black pall of coal-dust emanated from the Pelaw Main Staiths. In the bottom right elbow lies the tiny yard of R. B. Harrison, and Wood Skinner's Yard is by now occupied by International Paints at the base of the view. The influence of the 1960s is evidenced by the tower blocks. *UN*

Above This is a photograph that, for me, embodies the essential Tyneside of recent past; it was taken in December 1951 from above Moloney's Quay, Pelaw Main, with the rather infamous Staiths pub on the extreme left. It is difficult to describe adequately such a scene, but noteworthy features include the pit heaps, pithead wheels, terraced housing, steam tugs, steam dredgers, coal staiths, gas street lamps, a staith teeming coal, and a cobbled path with a cartwheel route. You'll find much more if you remember those days! The tug is the *Mildred*, the collier the *Aralizz*. *KG collection*

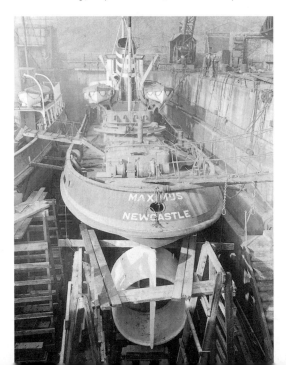

Left The *Maximus*, a German-built tug of 1956 vintage for the Ridley Steam Tug Co, was caught on this occasion dry-docked alongside a Batey Tug. The odd assembly around her stern, known as a Kort rudder, may or may not have been recently fitted, but as this is thought to be 1958 it is likely new. As luck would have it, she figures prominently throughout the book and it may be that the modification was successful. *JR*

Above right A rare wartime view of the hectic production process enforced upon British shipyards in an effort to maintain the status quo against U-boat casualties. This is the Vickers-Armstrong Naval Yard at Walker on the bend opposite Bill Quay. These slips, at 1,100 feet, allowed for the largest builds at the time, and were consequently in great demand. *UN*

Right Although the dock-gate under construction in the foreground was the photographer's target, it cannot be denied that he caught a moment of fascinating background activity as we see the side plating being fitted as an extension to the keel plates as a ship is born at the Naval Yard on a gloomy March day in the late 1950s. *SSG*

Left The Tyne's *Monarch of Bermuda* receives a post-war re-fit by Vickers-Armstrong at Low Walker in July 1948. Behind is the P&O liner *Strathaird* (which came with three funnels, and left with one!), and inside is company sister ship *Hertford*. *Laurence Dunn*

Right No Tyne album would be complete without some mention of *Turbinia*. Charles Parsons, born in 1854, spent his early years experimenting with engines in the search for perfection and at the age of 30 invented his first turbine. Five years later he formed his own company, and after a further six years formed the Steam Turbine Co and registered his patent.

Turbinia was built at the Brown & Hood Works, Wallsend, launched in August 1894 and engined from Parsons' own Heaton Works. At the Spithead Naval Review of 1897 she recorded 34.5 knots and ran rings around those attempting to stop this act of impudence in front of Royalty. Thenceforth orders for Parsons' famed engine rolled in and the first Admiralty order for HMS *Viper* in 1899 meant that he had arrived with full approval.

An accident occurred in 1907 when, at the launch of the *Crosby*, *Turbinia* was hit amidships, causing much damage. She was cut in half, the fore-section going to London. This was offered back to the City in 1944, was rejoined in 1959-61, and on 30 October 1994 she finally moved complete to a final resting place of her own – the Turbinia section of Newcastle's Discovery Museum at Blandford Street. This opened to the public in March 1996. *SSG/Tyne & Wear County Council Museums*

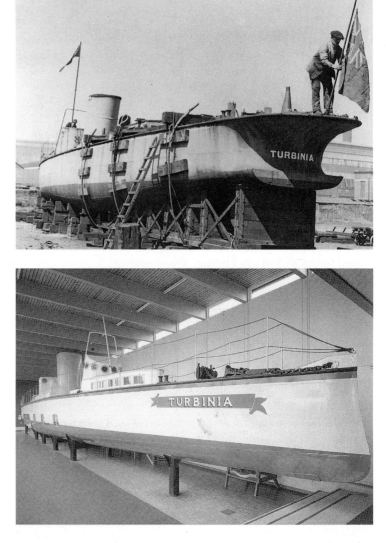

4. WALKER TO JARROW

O, ye taak aboot travels an' voyages far,
But thor's few beats the trip fre' the toon te the bar,
As ye gan doon te Tynemouth ye'll hear
the chep shoot -
'Here's Howdon for Jarrow, maa hinnies
loup oot. . .!

(From Richard Heslop's song 'Howdon
for Jarrow', popular about 1879)

A very large book would still not adequately describe the enormous maritime progress credited to the yards of this 2 miles of the riverfront. This stretch arguably saw the most prolific ship delivery machine concentration ever assembled in the Western World at its peak in the early years of the 20th century. We hardly go two paces before we are upon the site of John Coutts yard, which is credited with the construction of the first large iron ship on the river, the *Prince Albert* of 1842. This site became the Neptune Yard, founded in 1860 by John Wigham Richardson, and conveniently adjacent to Shaw's marine engine works. By 1903 this venture had joined forces with Swan Hunter, whose original yard was beyond the Hebburn/Wallsend ferry, and in terms of industrial muscle was echoed on the opposite shore by the 140-acre Palmers' site.

Strangely enough, Wallsend was originally better known throughout the world for its high-quality coal rather than ships. Johnson tells us:

'. . . in the late 1800s, Newcastle coal was ubiquitous, it was everywhere. European gas works, Indian mills, American railways, and coaling stations all over the world were fed with Newcastle coal. "West Hartley" was as familiar a term to the foreign buyer as was "Wallsend Main".'

As described in the Introduction, by the mid-19th century coal was receding from the riverfront scene, and metal and chemical works prospered for a short time. The Tharsis Copper Works was on the site of Willington Waggonway, but such was the pace of riverside evolution that this too disappeared to be replaced by the Willington (later Clelands) shipyards.

We can't move far before viewing something of Swan Hunter's empire. This extended to a working area of 80 acres, and today huge oil rig modules are built in the yards of its former maritime neighbours at Howdon. One of these sites was the Wallsend Slipway Company, where 'firsts' were a common occurrence. They produced the first steel boiler on the Tyne in 1878 and had the honour of fitting the steam turbines for the *Mauretania*. Closed in the mid-1980s, the site was cleared for oil rig construction.

In between various cement works (which were also receding by 1900) was the North Eastern Marine Engineering Company, specialising in engines for its shipbuilding neighbours from 1882. NEM's 'bread and butter' product was its triple-expansion steam machinery for 'tramps' and freighters large and small. Its huge electrically operated crane of 1909 (with a lifting capacity of 150 tons) was – and remains – a landmark seen from as far away as Morpeth. NEM became Clark-Hawthorn for a short time and latterly Clark Kincaid.

To the North of Clelands, the Hadrian Yard was the site of TIS – Tyne Iron Shipbuilding Co – and lay adjacent to another branch of the Charles Palmer Empire. Maritime enthusiasts may remember the standard and highly successful 'C' design ships that became TIS's trademark, and more than 1,500 were built under franchise by other yards.

Few years could equal the achievements of 1906 for maritime activity on this part of the Tyne. Nationally, things were changing. A new Liberal Government came to power and shipbuilding tonnage launched from the Tyne reached new heights. This year will be remembered, however, as the year that the Tyne received her greatest accolade (and challenge) – to build a major Cunard liner, the *Mauretania*.

Wallsend owes much to George Hunter for capturing this opportunity. His energetic directorship first smoothed the way towards amalgamation with the Wigham Richardson company, which resulted in the joint and successful bid. Let us also not forget the skill of the Tynesiders who carved her. The building of this fast and beautiful ship was a great and glorious achievement to the men who worked on her. Besides the complications of providing power, she was very much a 'one-off', and thus challenged the workmen with considerable difficulties as innovations were put to their first practical test. Nevertheless, *Mauretania* always performed

magnificently, reflecting Tyne shipbuilding ability at its finest.

After many low points in shipbuilding, the 1940s and the war years brought about changes that streamlined methods and shook Swan Hunter into good shape for the difficult 1950s. To illustrate this point, in 1940 world shipping output was 1.7 million tons, Britain being responsible for almost half of this. Ten years on, world output was 13.8 million tons, but Britain was producing only 8 per cent. This was not only the result of so much destruction in our ports and docks, but also a reflection of the 'conveyor-belt' style of production instituted by the USA. The Tyne still depended heavily upon traditional riveting techniques, and during the war the 54,000 shipyard workers in the North East produced 500 merchantmen. Swan Hunter built an incredible 83 warships at its Tyne and Clyde yards, but the world had moved on.

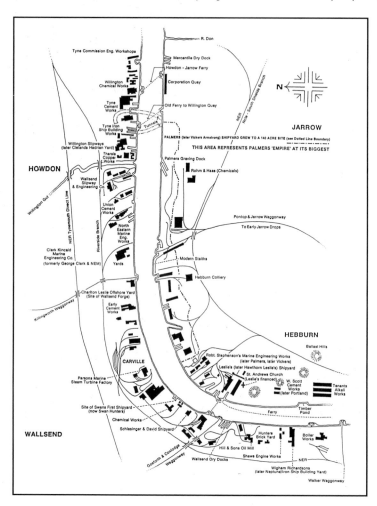

Left The Tyne: Walker to Jarrow

A 1975 aerial view of the main concentration of Wallsend builders from the Neptune Yard, below the camera, past Wallsend Dry Docks to the main Wallsend shipyards. Supertanker *Tyne Pride* dwarfs the Tyneside streets towards the top of the picture. Across the river is Hawthorn Leslie's site. *UN*

Across the river now, and to a site at the east end of Hebburn Quay came a Shetland crofter called Andrew Leslie who was determined to build iron ships. A protégé of Mitchell, Leslie formed a partnership with Coutts. The *Clarendon* was his first ship in 1854, and he showed dogged determination in the face of local Geordies who initially resented the Scots intrusion, but they soon came to admire and respect him. Some 264 ships went down his slipways before amalgamation with R. & W. Hawthorn in 1886. By 1890 the yard was building cruisers such as HMS *Bellona*, and in the 1920s ships for both P&O and Cunard. These orders helped the company to survive through a difficult spell and extended its reputation further, but by 1933 there was employment for only 650 men and just one vessel left the Hebburn slipway.

In 1937 fresh hope came with the order for HMS *Manchester*, while the following year saw the launch of HMS *Jervis* and HMS *Kelly*. Flotilla-leader *Kelly* (Ship No 615) was to capture the imagination of the nation under the command of Lord Louis Mountbatten when, in the words of the Naval Controller, she '. . . was got into harbour not only by the good seamanship of the Officers and men, but also on account of the excellent workmanship which ensured the watertightness of the other compartments'. *Kelly* had been towed off the Norwegian coast after being torpedoed on 8 May 1940. Her survival to fight another day astounded everyone who saw her condition in dry dock.

The yard's last ship, the 10,036-ton *Wiltshire* of 1968, closed this particular chapter in a fine maritime tradition. Below St Andrew's Church, a Tyne landmark, some cranes remain and the yard offices were lately a training centre for apprentices in shipbuilding. It would be good to think that ships may yet again be built at this historic location!

Moving along further brings us to Robert Stephenson's maritime adventure. His plant operated between 1886 and 1910, when a slump prompted a takeover by the neighbouring Palmer yard. Palmer later left this site to be taken under the wing of another familiar name, Vickers-Armstrong. Shipbuilding recommenced in 1939, in time to fit out *Jervis Bay* for her armed merchantman's role. In the 1950s almost £4 million was spent to bring the yard up to date, but

vessels still outgrew facilities and closure followed in 1970.

More staiths are passed before we come to perhaps the most incredible self-sufficient ship-manufacturing company on the river – Palmer's. It was here that Charles Palmer established a considerable reputation for fine merchantmen. However, in the early 1900s seven battleships were also constructed, including HMS *Lord Nelson*. She was virtually the last 'pre-Dreadnought' and was almost obsolete upon launch! This great shipyard began its decline in 1923 with the closure of its steelworks, and the National Securities Company closed the main yard in 1933 – to 'reduce UK shipbuilding capacity'.

The actual sites can be confusing – even to maritime experts! Palmers Shipbuilding & Iron Co started up at Jarrow in 1852. There was also a Palmers Steel & Iron Co yard operative at Howdon from 1860 to 1891, plus a Hebburn yard from 1911 to the end in 1933. Where the most confusion appears to creep in is after the 1933 crash, when the Hebburn site was taken over by Vickers and a new company formed, although not licensed to build ships. This became Palmers Hebburn Co Ltd, but was unconnected to the previous management. The dry docks were enlarged and increased over the years and everything went well after 1945, the company eventually becoming part of Swan's shipbuilding group.

These yards, then, will be remembered for the excellent working relationship between men and managers. Their closure rocked Hebburn and Jarrow as they accounted for 50 per cent of local employment. The famous Jarrow March of 1936 was a consequence of this dire situation.

Today the chemical company of Rohm & Hass occupies part of the eastern end of the former Palmers site and keeps quite a few chemical tankers busy at its quay, while Nissan has extended the Tyne's tradition of car transportation further to the east. Close by we find the only 'staith' operative, the coal-conveyor-belt-connected Tyne Coal Terminal. But don't get excited about it – it is perhaps visually one of the dullest sites on the river in comparison with its lineage down the years and sadly saw little activity in 1997.

The old course of the River Don forms the limit

to this section of the river; its new course, around Jarrow Slake, will be seen in the next chapter.

This digest of mostly long-gone activities in this area has barely scraped the surface; further reading by experts on their subject will be found in the Bibliography.

Considered by many as the most perfect of Cunard's liners, RMS *Mauretania* certainly brought fame and fortune to her Tyne builders, Swan, Hunter & Wigham Richardson. Launched on 20 September 1906, she included steam turbines never before attempted on this scale as well as many untried solutions to much untried technology in engineering technique. To say that she was ahead of her time is perhaps an understatement, and she dominated the Atlantic speed crossings from her very first run to New York in 1907. The rest of the maritime world began to catch up in the 1920s, but it was not until the arrival on the scene of the *Bremen* in 1929 that the Blue Riband was wrenched from her grasp. Even after this time she regularly produced improved performance, but failed by a whisker to wrest the crown back in 1933 – only two years away from her eventual retirement! After some cruise work in 1934 (in the white livery seen here) the hard decision was made to scrap her. In this view she bids farewell for ever to Tyneside witnessed by many dignitaries who made the journey off the Tyne to see her on her last journey to Rosyth. She will never be forgotten by Tynesiders. *SSL*

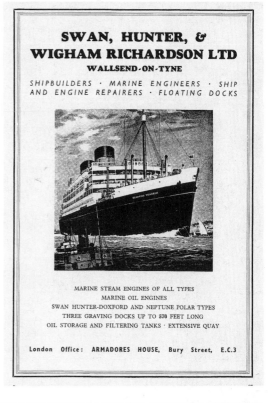

Below Meduana, one of two French liners built by Swan Hunter at Wallsend for service between Bordeaux and South America was launched on 30 September 1920. On 22 November, during fitting out, a fire was discovered on board, which resulted in the loss of two lives. A great deal of loose equipment is on board during the fitting-out process, and that didn't help when combined with the hundreds of gallons of water pumped on board. The result was instability and she keeled over at her fitting-out quay. Raised in April 1921, she entered service in November 1922, none the worse! *Swan Hunter Shipbuilding Ltd*

Below This busy mid-Tyne scene is set against the backcloth of the *Mauretania's* building shed. It is early 1944 and the programme to build as many large and strongly armed Destroyers as possible to compensate for losses is at its peak. The tug *Wearmouth* makes cautious progress up river towing the *Titan II* crane between five partially completed examples of Tyne-built Battle Class destroyers. They include HMS *Barfleur*, HMS *Armada*, HMS *Trafalgar*, HMS *Sole Bay* and HMS *St Kitts*. They were, however, too late to play an active part in the war, but gave excellent service with NATO in later years, many finding their way back to North East ports for breaking-up in the late 1960s. *UN*

Right Not all of Swan's ten slipways at Wallsend had the latest facilities by the late 1930s. An anonymous ship completes in a wooden cocoon, while steel plating is on hand everywhere. *UN*

Below A late wartime view of a cluttered Swan Hunter dry dock. The atmosphere may well give an impression of a resigned complacency that the fire-fighting days of 'patch and plug' would seemingly never end. On the left is Bowring's *Regent Panther*, built at Swans during 1937-38, which enjoyed better fortune than her two sisters, *Regent Lion* and *Regent Tiger*, which were both war losses. She served her country well right up until the end of her own long campaign and went to Briton Ferry for breaking in October 1959. *UN*

Above For many Tynesiders the river lay dormant until 1968 when 'skyscraper' ships began to dwarf the surroundings, attracting much attention from everyone far and wide. *Esso Northumbria* was the first of four years' worth of such big builds, laid in April 1968. Ian Carr's picture shows her on the eve of her launch, 2 May 1969. After trials in February 1970 she was handed over to the Esso Petroleum Co in May of that year, never to visit Tyneside again. *Ian Carr*

Left To allow for the first of the new era of supertankers, Swans very much relied upon the cooperation of Hebburn Council to re-profile the opposite bank to facilitate this 253,000-ton launch. Here we see the new shape of things, with dredgers already hard at it in August 1968. *SSG*

Above Three years after HRH Princess Anne launched *Esso Northumbria* she returned to send *World Unicorn* on her impressive way on 3 May 1973. The view from the fitting-out cranes at Wallsend emphasises the amount of loose equipment involved in the final stages of completion. She was completed a year after the launch, and sadly (in view of the effort that went into producing her) went to an early scrapyard in Taiwan in 1984. Further down the river, amidst the murk, Swan's floating Titan crane assists repair work over at Hebburn. *UN*

Right *Tyne Pride* (seen from the air on page 63) is seen on the launch pad at Wallsend as Swan Hunter's Yard No 63, shortly before slipping into her natural element in early October 1975. Tugs are at standby on the extreme left. As a speculative build by the joint venture company Swan Maritime, she didn't retain this name long. Eventually sold to Liberia, she became *Opportunity*, later again becoming the French-owned *Thermidor*, and finally and currently is the *New Resource* still trading on oil routes throughout the world. She was the heaviest ship ever constructed on the river, a record that seems likely now to stand for ever! Her 262,000 tons deadweight would have broken most river records! *UN*

Above The final touches are applied to HMS *Illustrious* at Swan Hunter's fitting-out quay at Walker shortly after her launch in 1978. She continued a great tradition of Tyne-built carriers and was one of three ordered in the 1970s to replace the then aging fleet of through-deck carriers. *KG*

Left Another view alongside Swan's Walker quay shows a final moment of international cooperation that was once a familiar cornerstone of the North East economy and could be said to have begun with Armstrong's 'Cruiser' exports a century before. Ahead of an almost completed HMS *Illustrious* lies the Iranian naval replenishment vessel *Kharg*. The story of *Kharg*'s start in life is interesting. She was launched in 1977 and completed in 1979, but could not be delivered until a certain 'slot' appeared in the political climate then obtaining. The Iranian crew numbers dwindled awaiting the granting of the export licence, which was eventually given in 1982 – when a refit was about due! *KG*

Left HMS *Chatham* at the Neptune Yard on 20 January 1988 prior to her launch. This yard had been in use since 1860, but this was to be its last build. *Swan Hunter Shipbuilding Ltd*

Right A sleepy moment on a lazy Sunday afternoon in September 1980 catches the Mid Tyne Ferry *Tyne Princess* laid up against a pontoon having collected two trawlers for company. This crossing point was a life-line for many shipyard workers at Hebburn when work dried up there, enabling them to cross easily to north-bank yards without incurred longer mileage costs. It conveniently operated to Swan's doorstep and survived into the late 1980s. *KG*

Below Tyneside was best known for saying 'adieu' to ships that rarely saw Britain's shores again, but an unusual turn-around forced upon the shipbuilders was the need to become skilled in shipbreaking to maintain some chance of employment continuity in the worst of the 1930s depression. Just such an opportunity came about with the arrival of Belfast-built *Olympic*, sister-ship to the infamous *Titanic*. Bought by Sir John Jarvis MP, her destruction helped to feed many hundreds of Jarrow people and her arrival on this sombre day in October 1935 left river folk unsure whether to cheer or cry. *SSL*

Left This much-copied picture dating back to circa 1880 gives a flavour of shipyard conditions at that time. The graving dock belongs to the age of sail and the vessel, *Switzerland*, constructed for the Red Star Line 20 years earlier by Palmers, reflecting a time when shipbuilders were hedging their bets by incorporating features old and new and coming up with vessels that weren't quite sure if they were steam or sail. *World Ship Society*

Below On the stocks at Hawthorn Leslie's Hebburn Yard in 1957 is the oil tanker *British Courage*. One of the trickiest and very precise jobs on the river at launch time is being performed by the dumb barge. Her swan-neck jib is helping to lay the drag-chains and their moorings, work that was done to shipyard calculations. It goes without saying that there was little tolerance either way, and no second try! Countless other jobs are being done around her by workers who appear ant-sized by comparison. *JJ*

If we feel inclined to criticise the technical merits of this view, we should instead be thankful that some enterprising soul produced anything at all, considering the weight of camera equipment and the scarcity of helicopters in 1928! We are looking east from towards the top of the map on page 62, and it would take many pages to describe all that can be seen. The centre of attraction has to be the big 'cradles' of Palmers Yard on the right. A large ship is close to launch while a 'Palmers Destroyer' completes alongside and another fits-out at the river berth. Just beyond, a ferry pulls away from Jarrow's Ferry Street terminal to proceed over to the Howdon landing stage off Stephenson Street. Above Palmers, railway tentacles

touch everywhere in and around the works of the New Jarrow Steel Co and Jarrow Metal Industries, both busy supplying shipyard demands. Below Palmers is a gas works and next is the ship-repairing yard of Mercantile Dry Dock, inundated by cargo-weary vessels. Jarrow Slake and the Shellmex oil terminal are at the top right.

On the opposite bank are the enclosed Northumberland Dock 'staithlands' and nearer the camera the slipways of the short-lived Northumberland Shipbuilding Co yard (1928), and the indent of the TIC workshops area. The rest is simply for visual enjoyment of a frozen moment in the Tyne's history. SSG

Above This 1976 aerial view is slightly further upstream than the previous one, and shows one of the longest straight sections of the river at Wallsend, at the point where the Willington Quay Gut runs into the Tyne after skirting the rope works of Hood Haggies and passing below two railway routes. This section saw the densest concentration of shipbuilding on the Tyne. From the top left bank downwards is the Tyne Improvement Commission Repair Yard. Then comes the former Clelands yard (founded in 1867), which had then been taken over by the Hadrian Yard. Across the Gut and with a bulk loader in dry dock is the Wallsend Slipway & Engineering Co yard, while almost immediately below the camera is the Clark Kincaid Marine Engineering Works.

On the opposite bank was then the NCB-owned-and-run Jarrow Staith and often a location for colliers to top-up on a short-fall in payload. Beyond this Rohm & Haas Chemicals complete a fascinating glimpse into another stopped river moment. *UN*

Left Tyne Improvement Commission officials take their annual 'jolly', officially their annual review of the river, upon their steam launch *Sir William Stephenson*, flying the TIC standard and a red duster at the stern. The tanker *British Chivalry* provides an awesome backcloth here in the middle reaches of the Tyne. *JJ*

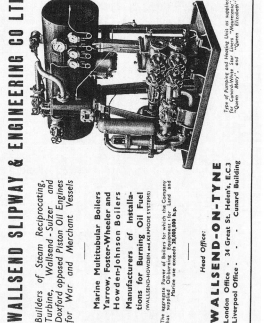

The moment when a supertanker bids farewell to her place of birth. Weighing in at 126,539 tons gross, *Esso Hibernia* was in the middle of a batch produced during the 1970-76 period when oil demand was high and prices fluctuating. Many went early for scrapping, some a mere five years after being built. She is shown here skirting the area formerly part of Palmer's extensive shoreline. It can be seen that wasteland still swamps the growing number of burgeoning new factory units. *UN*

INTERLUDE: TYNE PORTRAITS

Right Simply a photograph no longer possible, but well remembered. Newcastle Quayside, 1956. *JJ*

Below The ancient Quayside viewed from South Shore Road, Gateshead, December 1959. *NCL*

Raw beauty 'twixt Wallsend and Jarrow, 1954. SSG

Above A dramatic skyline of shipyard dinosaurs and a strong swell running into Tyne Dock, 1956. *JJ*

Below Awaiting their turn. . . Four 'old salts' line up at the Tyne Dock Engineering Co repair yard, South Shields, 1959. *JJ*

Left The City glimpsed from Friars Goose Shore, Felling, 1967. *KG*

Left, inset France Fenwick's tugs *Beamish* and *Hendon* take their ease at the end of the working day off the Bergen Quay, April 1959. *JJ*

Above *Redgate* and *Gloxinia* under Mercantile Dockyard cranes. *SSL*

Below In the late 1940s *Fulham* wallows in a choppy river breeze along with other 1920s/'30s colliers off Dunston. Fulham Borough Council ordered eight colliers of the same name prefixed by their order number (this *Fulham* was the first, thus unnumbered). Fulham power station was unusual in having no other delivery source but waterway, hence the eventual large number of ten ships that bore this name. Retired from the coal run in 1958, she was broken up in Holland in the same year. *UN*

Top left The work of the 'little ships' over, *Empress of England* leaves her birthplace to fend for herself upon the ocean's of the world. *JJ*

Middle left Possibly the 'sharpest'-looking of all frequent Tyne visitors was Fred Olsen's *Blenheim* (Thornycroft's yard, Southampton, 1951). She has an ageless appeal. Shields, 1958. *JJ*

Bottom left Always a stirring sight, *Northern Star* with her sexy sheer is cajoled on her way out to sea by perhaps superfluous Tyne tugs in 1961. *JJ*

Shipyard cradles, Wallsend, 1982. *KG*

Left Teeming gear at rest, Dunston Staiths, 1978. KG

Right Sun and shadows amidst the cobbled yards of Elswick Works. This was the secretive world of 'Dreadnought' construction, still in this condition in 1969. KG

Below Sun and shadow above Dunston and *Fulham X* (1948-70), 1959. JJ

5. HOWDON TO PERCY MAIN

I have seen the old ships
Sail like Swans asleep
Beyond the village which men still call Tyre
With leaden age o'er cargoed, Dipping Deep
For Famagusta and the hidden Sun. . .'

(From 'The Old Ships' by James Flecker, 1884-1915)

The Tyne Improvement Commission certainly made its presence felt on this corner of the river and transformed it within seven years of the Commission's inauguration. In 1928 the TIC invited the Duke of Northumberland to an area that had once been open fields (below an obscure colliery village called Percy Main) to open Northumberland Docks. Soon, 50 per cent of the output from the Blyth and Tyne area pits was making for the dock and, as seen on the map opposite, they may have shared 'metals' but they nevertheless divided to their respective colliery staiths for teeming to 'dedicated' trading partners (Ships Masters generally knew their staith!). Their product was the best-quality steam coal or bunker coal, and the docks soon became popular also for 'topping up' the bunkers of passing steamers.

Prior to this the pits' only other outlet had been via small private harbours at Seaton Sluice and Blyth. At the latter the water depth was still at this time such that only ships of limited burthen could load. Consequently foreign trade suffered badly, until the advent of Northumberland Dock. This brings us to a maritime story as reported in the *Newcastle Daily Chronicle* of 4 December 1901, but referring to an event of 1842:

'The Bedlington Coal Company had just adopted a novel method of shipping their coals in the Tyne. Loaded chaldron waggons, 40 at a time, were conveyed by an iron twin-screw steamer *Bedlington*, especially constructed for the purpose, from the staiths on the north side of the river Blyth . . . to Shields Harbour on the Tyne. They were there discharged into colliers by means of steam derricks with which the vessel is provided.'

The difficulties of competing logistically with collieries having direct Tyne access can be seen to have driven some entrepreneurial Northumbrians to imaginative answers, and one has to applaud their determination and the fact that they had, in effect, preempted containerisation by 120 years! Incidentally, the *Bedlington*, built at Marshall's (South Shields), was sold in April 1851 for service as a ferry on the Forth. It was another four years before the 'Northumberland Dock and Percy Main Branch Railway Act' was passed under the guidance of that railway scoundrel, George Hudson.

The TIC eventually became involved with railway operations and it can be seen on the map that it had its own Commissioners Railway system, which included its own signal boxes, staff and engines, some examples of which will be noted in these pages. The TIC maintained the tracks to Hayhole Point and Whitehill Point Staiths and eventually, with the advent of the docks at Albert Edward, extended its system in 1928 to its own Tyne Commissioners Quay and a passenger service connection with North Sea ferries. This service still operates today, but the surroundings are perhaps the least inspiring of the current maritime scene along the Tyne.

The Northumberland Docks are now completely filled in to the breakwater line on the map. The Hayhole Lead Works remains as an inhospitable island amidst wasteland where lorry trailers accumulated, but the hinterland storage wastes have since been rejuvenated by such things as the Royal Quays shoppers' paradise and the

'Wet and Wild' pool complex for children. The Albert Edward Dock survives and still passes cars for export.

Whitehill Point last saw coal shipments in 1974 and the site is now unrecognisable. Adjacent to the old lock gates at Howdon was the Tyne Tanker Cleaning Company, helping reduce pollution in the environment.

We now turn our attention to that area of High Shields across the river downstream of Tyne Dock where, thanks to historian Amy Flagg, we know a lot more about the beginnings of early shipbuilding. Many thought that the docks adjacent to Potts Quay were the first, but in her book she tells us:

'. . .legend [says] that the first dock in the town was built by the Wallis family on the

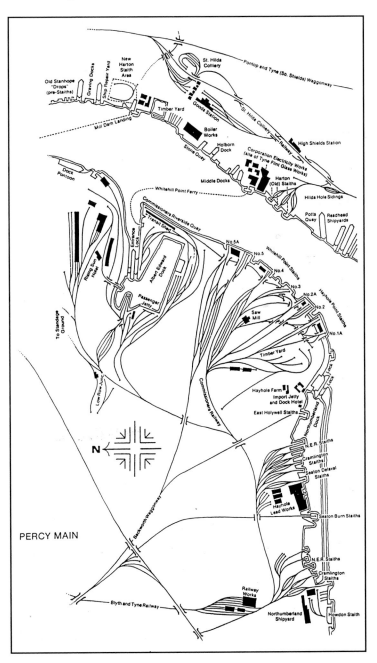

Right The Tyne: Howdon to Percy Main

site occupied . . . by John Readhead & Son, and known as the West Docks. The dock constructed by John, Thomas and William Wallis was the High Dock at the junction of Commercial Road and West Holborn, and occupied for many years by the related firms of Straker, Edward's and Smith; and, in any case, it was not the first dock in the town, this honour [falling] to the Low Dock in Wapping Street.'

These West Docks are shown as 'Readhead Shipyards' on our map, and, she adds, '. . .were planned, laid out and occupied on agricultural land by a Sunderland firm in 1811. Potts Quay, nearby, was eventually built into for a dock [and in 1822] was sold by Mr James Young to Messrs Readhead & Co, iron shipbuilders. . .'

So began a story that lasted into the 1990s, their first ship, the *Jane Kilsall*, being launched in January 1882.

Further along a little to Middle Docks and No 1 Dock is the original facility of about 1768 (although much enlarged). The first Middle Dock Company built small wooden ships up to 1899, when it became the Middle Dock & Engineering Company, hard up against the Mill Dam. The No 3 Dock was built to 460 feet and extended into the Holborn Dock following the departure of Eltringham & Co. In more modern times, Readhead's are remembered for their long associations with such shipping lines as Haines, Runciman's and Strick Line. In 1968 they became another 'arm' of Swan Hunter, but in 1970 shipbuilding became ship repair only.

The Stone Quay, originally built for shipping limestone from the quarries at Cleadon, was the centre of a group of salt-pans in mid-18th century. About 1878 Mr J. T. Eltringham acquired the site and for ever after it became associated with the boatyard. The company had begun the Middle Landing area and was very well known at the turn of the century for its fine paddle-steamers, tugs and, later, steam trawlers; the *Cullercoats* illustrated on page 94 is a fine example of Eltringham longevity! By 1907 the yard had built 26 trawlers for the Prince Fishing

Company of North Shields, but one of the best-known ships was the tug *Great Emperor*. She was built for John Dry Steam Tugs in 1909 and eventually passed to Messrs France, Fenwick of Newcastle. On 5 February 1959 the *Shields Gazette* reported:

'This week has seen the passing of one of the Tyne's oldest steam tugs, the *Great Emperor*. She is now at King's Yard at Gateshead, for breaking up. When she was built fifty years ago at the Eltringham Yard she was regarded as the pride of the Tyne tugs and looked upon as such for many years; but [she] has been lying idle and out of service for the past eight weeks and now she comes under the breakers' hammers. . .'

Some other lasts: exactly 11 years earlier a similar sad postscript appeared in the *Newcastle Weekly Chronicle* when the last of our sailing ship visitors suddenly appeared at King's scrapyard at Gateshead. '. . .The *Archibald Russell*, now but a hulk, is tied up in a Tyne scrapyard, the last of her kind on the river. . .'

A final obituary was a comment by the paper's shipping correspondent in 1924 when the last collier brig came up to Gateshead looking a very sorry sight and bringing an end to the 'Tyne armada'.

'Hundreds of people hurrying on their way to work over the Tyne Bridge must have looked at an old wooden ship lying forlorn on the shore at Gateshead without realising that she represents the last of the collier brigs, the little vessels which laid the foundation of the prosperity of the North East coast. . . The vessel now at Gateshead where she is being broken up is none other than the *Vindex*. She has lain for years off Howdon Dock Wall as a coal hulk owned by Purdy of North Shields. . .'

However, generally recognised as last of the Tyne collier brigs was the *Remembrance*. She was built at Middlesbrough in 1865 and was lost in 1904. It therefore appears that *Vindex* had been in use as a hulk for some considerable time!

By the time of this 1976 aerial photo, the timber staithland of Howdon/Northumberland Dock was well on its way back towards the landscape that features again here today. Central to the photograph is the Tyne Tunnel that displaced the ferry seen in the earlier aerial view. The entrance is below the conical funnel as the road doubles back upon itself; the smaller circular building, nearer the river, is the pedestrian tunnel. Scarred areas show cleared sites where once hundreds of miles of railway sidings criss-crossed the area. A small area of water is the last piece of the old coal dock. Some extant railway is seen leading to the Percy Main Esso terminal – the last rail customer where there were once hundreds. UN

Above A wide spectrum of activity is seen down the line in this middle river view at Howdon Staith in 1959. John Hudson Fuel & Shipping Co's vessels were always a feature of the '50s river scene. *Hudson Strait* was completed in 1946 at Troon, no doubt containing a wide montage of many other broken-up vessels! She became *Camelina* in 1967 and was broken up in 1975. The well-cared-for wooden bridge sections were another feature of this group of ships, and many local men sailed them. *JJ*

Below Parked behind *Hudson Strait* on the same day was *Firelight*, which could be described as a fearless survivor of London's 'coal scuttle brigade'. Her name, far from prompting some trivial or humorous comment, was almost her badge of honour, describing how her actions *did* in fact keep many of the home fires burning through the terrible Blitz days. She began life at Burntisland in 1943 and her paint was barely dry when, on 4 November of that year, her bows were blown off by an E-vessel near Cromer outward-bound from London to the Tyne. Her new bow was fitted in a South Shields yard and she survived to go on to have many more narrow squeaks. In 1953 she collided with Grimsby trawler *Rivier* off Flamborough Head; the sad result was the loss of ten lives. She was eventually sold out of the North Thames Gas business in 1964 to end her days as a storage barge in Norway. *JJ*

This 1976 view adjoins the top of that on page 89, and looks down on what was once the Northumberland Dock coal basin, showing that events have gone full circle. However, the topography cannot disguise its previous role and the ghost 'fans' of lifted sidings are easily traceable. Prominent is the then still rail-connected Esso oil terminal, with a pipeline running down to a river berth. A solitary coaster lies moored to the dolphins at a Whitehill Point that is also still rail-connected. The land-fill of the coal dock, also seen in later photographs, is almost complete, and only the Associated Lead Works (at the bottom of the picture) has a small riverfront, while in the old dock area are now Velva Liquids and the Tank Cleaning Co. *UN*

Top A look at the early shape of things inside Northumberland Dock, once referred to as Howdon Dock, with the boom barrier just visible to the right. The dock was the channel for the produce of the likes of Seaton Delavel, Cramlington and many more pits in south-east Northumberland, and the staith seen here was a lead-off from the Cramlington waggonway. These early staith constructions bring to mind the American trestle bridges of 'western' films, and there's a possibility that they frequently used Oregon pine in their construction. Northumberland Dock was unusual in having individual single staiths for each of the private owners running in from the pits of Northumberland. This would almost certainly be due to the high tonnages shipped, but may also have had something to do with the jealous nature of rival pit factions. *Ernie Brack*

Middle A detail of the Cramlington Staith top circa 1920, showing the way that empties could bypass loaded inward-bound wagons where the lines split. The camera is above the coal holes leading to the chutes that teemed directly to the waiting ships on either side. *Ernie Brack*

Bottom We are now overlooking the Northumberland Dock lock gates, pump houses and canal entrance. In the right background is a now strangely quiet coal dock in its final moments and dotted with redundant buoys. The isolation of this corner above Whitehill Point and its juxtaposition to the Shellmex-BP Jarrow oil terminal made this an ideal location for a tanker cleaning facility. The need for relative isolation resulted from the occasions when explosions occurred following a build-up of volatile fumes in empty tanks. Inevitably this was a little-photographed area of the river. *JJ*

Top With changing coal-moving methods from the Northumberland pits, Northumberland Dock lost its usefulness, although neighbouring Whitehill Point continued to teem coal right up to 1974. The infilling of the dock presented an opportunity to extend already less socially acceptable industrial processes adjacent to the already polluted Associated Lead Works site. Here we see work progressing in difficult and barren conditions in October 1958, with the boom now breached. Howdon Staith is in action behind. *NCL*

Middle The infilling saw the beginning of the first major return to a river shape close to the original profile of 1840. Northumberland Dock contained only twisted stumps of disused foreshortened staiths when Harbour & General Works gangs began work in the autumn of 1958. *NCL*

Bottom High tide affords a good overall view of the same location a little later on in the process. Associated Lead is shrouded in November mists, while a boom mooring dolphin forms the anchor. *NCL*

Top A bird's-eye view of Hayhole Point Staiths and two flat-iron power colliers lying up in wait of coal in 1965. The arc spans of the two distribution spouts are seen together with the now truncated leads to the old wooden jetties. *UN*

Middle Another view at Hayhole Point, with *Sir William Walker* receiving minerals from Northumberland in 1960. She was another product of Austin & Pickersgill's Wear yard for the Central Electricity Authority. Built in 1954, she ended her days in 1983 after having conveyed well in excess of three million tons of coal along the way! *JJ*

Bottom One of Stephenson, Clarke's traders, the *Steyning*, built by Austin & Pickersgill in 1955 and engined by George Clark, also on the Wear, lies alongside Hayhole Point Staiths. France Fenwick's tug *Cullercoats* is also alongside, and is a particular example of longevity. She was launched in 1898 from Rennoldson Yard at South Shields, and went on to serve in the Anchor Line for 70 years, carrying only one other name, *Cyclops*, for a short time. She was broken up at Dunston in 1968 at a time when preservation wasn't even considered. *JJ*

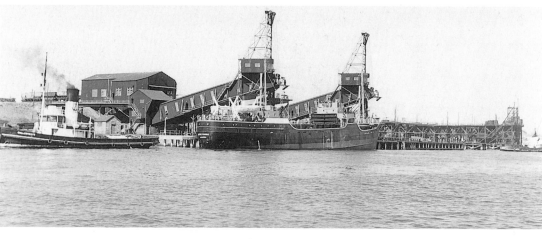

This quite superb Tyne view dated 20 April 1965 shows *British Craftsman* going to sea, under tow, past the staiths at Whitehill Point. In the foreground awaiting a berth is the collier *John Orwell Phillips*. This ship was built on the neighbouring River Wear by Pickersgill & Sons in 1955 and served the North Thames Gas Board. She made many visits to Tyne staiths until her sale to Panamanian interests in 1968. *SSG*

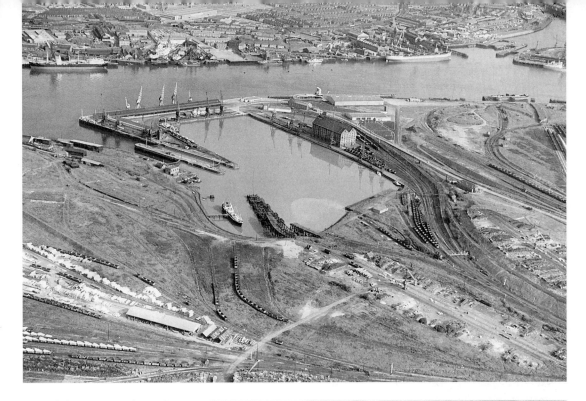

Above left We now take to the air
again, and cumulus cloud floats like
candy-floss over North Shields while
white horses charge into the sandy bays
off South Shields on this July day in
1971. Some details seen along the
winding Tyne include Albert Edward
Dock just right of centre and oil storage
tanks close to Percy Main. The
foreground housing estates include
Meadowwell. The coast of Seaham and
Durham County itself recedes into the
horizon of more clouds. *UN*

Left Swinging round to the west we are
now looking down on to the entrance
of both Albert Edward Dock (top
centre) and Tyne Dock (bottom right).
Readhead's Yard, with three dry docks
and a ship, is also seen on the extreme
right. Towards the bottom of the

picture are the tanks of the Tanker Cleaning Co adjacent to
the now completely filled in Northumberland Dock with
new industries in place. Even this view of 1976 is far
removed from today's scene. Sadly, it is a bonus now if you
see shipping activity anywhere along the river. On a recent
visit to South Shields only the tugs *Selby Cross* and *Seasider*
were seen, while the Brigham Dock was being filled in. *UN*

Top Another aerial view from the north showing again
Albert Edward Dock with Tyne Dock top right; the details
inside the former are more closely studied in later pictures.
This 1974 view graphically shows an area struggling with the
loss of traditional industries and about to go through a deal

of painful metamorphosis, eventually levelling out in today's
'Millennium' climate of heavy funding. A blackened staith
stands alone like a rotten tooth (seen again below), the last
about to fall in a scene once heavily populated with all the
props that go with concentrated railways, shipping and
mining. *UN*

Above The north-west corner of Albert Edward Dock,
showing what may have been described as the Oslo Quay
area in the 19th century. A tramp coaster is laid up at the
bridged dolphin and long forgotten railway wagons lie
abandoned, their former duties passed to the age of
containerisation. *UN*

Left Possibly seen at the turn of the last century, this three-master was thought to be loading coal in Tyne Dock, but when the *South Shields Gazette*'s 'Waterfront' column ran the picture in 1986, it was identified by George McGuire, an ex-teemer and trimmer, as a ship at the Oslo Quay Staith inside Albert Edward Dock. He also added that he remembered the last sailing ship to leave the Tyne as being the *Peru*, of Swedish owners. He said that she had left with 1,000 tons of hard coke for Australia before 1914. This unidentified beauty shows us clearly her 'cutty sark' lines and gold leaf signatory. *SSG*

Top Inside Albert Edward Dock a Tribal Class Destroyer awaits disposal instructions laid-up at dolphins where once colliers stood awaiting coal. A high and proud steam collier of an earlier age is at the south quay while on the far side one of Gresley's 'V' Class tank locomotives is impatiently blowing at the safety valves at the head of a Tyne Commission Quay train for King's Cross. We can thank John Johnson for taking the trouble to record unfashionable areas of Tyneside at a time when many changes beckoned. *JJ*

Above For the link to the Tyne Commissioners Quay on the through trains to and from King's Cross, Heaton Depot supplied these hardy 'V1' tank locos, which had fairly major gradients to overcome on sometimes heavy trains. Here we see two such examples on the quay sidings prior to loading London-bound services in May 1954. Steam-raising for the 8.40 am service is No 67646, while sister engine No 67651 awaits time with the stock for the 9.10 departure. The Bergen and Olsen line passengers usually only required Newcastle or London destinations, and in 1939 the only intermediate call was at Walkergate station, and only if requested by anyone! *R. K. Taylor*

Above This picture was taken from the top of a hydraulic coal hoist – subsequently replaced by the car customs terminal building seen in the photograph below. It may have been taken to show off the new electric cranes along the quay. A Tyne Improvement Commission red duster flutters above the TIC quay transit shed on this warm sunny June day in 1937, just nine years after the quay's completion. The newness is still apparent in the walkways, but the quietness is also alarming and men sit around idle – as do the few vessels on show. To the left Albert Edward Dock of the 1880s is also quiet. It saw one of the first major applications of hydraulic machinery, for powering the dock gates. *NSL*

Left Lifting of redundant embedded track goes on while the good ship *Venus* starts the swinging procedure behind a motor tug, inward-bound to Bergen. She started as the *Lubeck* for joint ownership by Bergen and Fred Olsen. She became the *Black Prince* for winter cruise duties on the London-Canaries run, reverting to her original role in summer. The smaller 1946-built Bergen Line *Mercur* awaits her turn. This photograph makes an interesting comparison with the earlier one above. *JJ*

Above In 1956 Bergen Line's *Leda* pokes her distinctive funnel above the customs shed as rows of Austin products assemble to await export. A large vessel awaits repair at Readhead's yard across the river. *JJ*

Below A product of Swan, Hunter & Wigham Richardson, *Leda* was built in 1952 incorporating two double-reduction-geared steam turbines constructed by the neighbouring Wallsend Slipway Company. Ready for the journey back home, her 6,670 tons are turned with assistance from Ridley's tug *Maximus*. Commonly referred to by Tynesiders as Norwegian mail steamers, these vessels were more than that and built up strong links with our Norse friends, many of which continue today. *JJ*

This 1958 Albert Edward Dock view underlines the importance of timber to the economics of northern ports, which helped establish companies such as Pyman Bell of Tyne Dock. The industry was supplied with thousands of tons of timber over the years, a great percentage coming from Finland and much supplied via the fleet of ships owned by the Bore family of Slottesgatam. These ships varied enormously, and featured here is *Bore IX*. Built by MacMillan's on the Clyde in 1910 as the *Queensbury*, she came to the Bore family in 1921 and was their biggest ship at the time. She lasted for one more trading year and arrived in Hong Kong for breaking on 27 May 1959. *JJ*

Right At the end of the 1990s cars remain as the main commercial activity of the working Tyne. This is 1959 and we were then exporting Austin Westminster and Cambridge models. The Spanish-built *El Salazar*, owned by Nav Del Atlanticos, is embarking a cargo of salt at Albert Edward Dock. *JJ*

Below This late 1950s view of the north-west corner of Albert Edward dock throws up a rich harvest of industrial detail. Ruston-built TIC diesel shunter No 35 is buffering on to a rake of wooden wagons long since past their main-line sell-by date, but nevertheless usefully employed internally. The high embankment separating this Coble Dene area from Northumberland Dock conveyed railways on to the staiths at Hayhole Point where the coal anti-breakage assembly can be seen beyond the TIC signal box. The unidentified foreign coaster appears to be have almost discharged its load of pit props. This would surely make a fascinating period piece for modellers! *JJ*

Tyne Dock

The Stanhope & Tyne Railway first built coal drops (as shown in the top left-hand corner of the map on page 87) just east of the Harton 'new' staiths of today. Their modest facilities were clearly ill-conceived and, together with copious land purchased along the Stone Quay area by the Brandling Railway Company, were all aborted when the Stanhope & Tyne Railway went bankrupt and that company's own plans for a massive coal-shipping dock was similarly aborted.

A Tyne Dock Company was formed on 1 July 1839 by an Act of Parliament, and this scheme was eventually developed by the NER. Excavations for the dock were suspended in 1849 and a new Act was obtained in 1854, including even more enlarged facilities. In January 1859 coal finally started to pass through the dock, and, as will be seen from the accompanying map, it was constructed on the eastern fringe of that area known as Jarrow Slake, in parts a bleak place even today.

Designed for the NER by local engineer Mr T. Harrison, Tyne Dock was declared the largest coal dock in the world and certainly remained so until the late 19th century. Its main basin consisted of a 50-acre area and four main jetties, supplemented by numerous smaller 'spouts' and cargo-handling berths. At the time of planning it was (bearing in mind the average size of the sailing vessels then predominant in the coal trade) intended to accommodate up to 500 vessels.

When the coal began to flow, it meant that all the slow one-wagon spouts became extinct and the colliers no longer had to wait for a week at a time at the buoys in the coal queue. The Tyne 'coal-rush' had begun, and as fast as shipbuilders produced colliers, Londoners begged for even more. The coal-owners continually raised the keel-rates and the shipping agents/owners similarly profited from the trade. The overall Tyne shipment figure in 1859 was 4 million tons; this jumped to more than 10 million tons by 1890, and reached a peak in excess of 21 million tons in 1923, before industrial strife laid low river produce.

By 1934 Tyne Dock had shipped an incredible 323 million tons of coal, an astounding figure. The rails to the staiths passed over a busy road at their 'neck' and this noisy black tunnel was known to generations as the 'arches'. Beyond were 25 miles of sidings, all of which passed over to the Tyne Improvement Commission in 1938. Our photographs depict the Dock through to 1965, when infilling got under way.

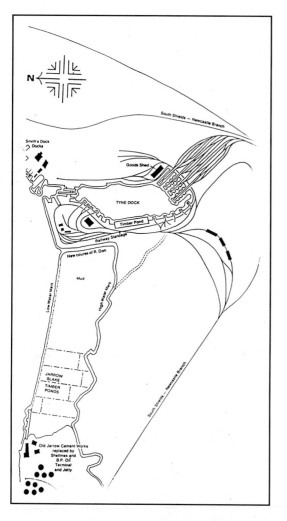

Left Tyne Dock and Jarrow Slake

Above right A view of the south end of Tyne Dock. This 200-acre Dock Estate, with 49 acres under water, was formed in 1859 and was taken over by the Tyne Improvement Commission from the LNER (successor to the NER) in 1938. This method of timber berthing is examined in more detail elsewhere. UN

Right This 1976 aerial view incorporates the entire area of the accompanying map, and quite a lot more! We see here the more recent fate of Tyne Dock – gone now are the eight warehouses, and the two transit sheds have been modified for the new era of timber trading. The area at the top of the picture shows that all rail connections have been lifted, leaving a large amount of white wood visible from the air. It is heartening that in 1976 here, at least, some vessels were busy at the remaining cranes of the North West Quay, the

original ore quay. An ore carrier is at the new Ore Quay in the river, and opposite a collier loads during the eleventh hour of mineral exporting from Hayhole Point Staith. The ro-ro vessel, top left, is at the Tyne Commissioner's Quay. In the foreground several vessels lie at the BP Quay (associated oil storage tanks are close by St Paul's tiny church, once the home of St Bede). In between Jarrow Slake is rapidly becoming terra firma for the then fast approaching Tyne Coal Terminal construction. Today it is the last coal exporting outpost along what were the 20 coaly miles of the Tyne. Note how the Tyne Dock 'arches' (where a road passed beneath the staith approaches) are left as four stumps of shored wall with a waste disposal plant where the sidings once lay. *UN*

Below This iron-hulled three-masted collier displaying a frightening demon below its bowsprit is believed to be inside Tyne Dock circa 1890 at a primitive coal-loading device that hardly qualifies to be called a staith. A five-plank 13-ton NER wagon and heavy hoist buckets are two of the interesting details above, while at water level a foyboatman appears to be marshalling up loose timber. *Auty Collection, NCL*

Bottom This interesting old photograph of Tyne Dock dated about 1922 is a flashback to the days when North East ports were a constant forest of masts and funnels of all shapes and sizes. This was at the peak of coal exporting, and that year Tyne Dock alone recorded a figure of 6½ million tons of coal. In total that year 19 million tons of coal and coke left the river – only bettered in 1923, with an all-time peak of 21½ million tons. Providing a permanent record of such output from our local mines are pictures such as this. Prominent is the *Schieland* built in 1916 by Smulders. She survived the First World War to become a victim of the Second. The vessel to the left is *Gertrude Salling*; she was built by T. & W. Smith as the *Dunstanborough* back in 1871 and received her new name in 1922, possibly just weeks before this picture, from her new owner, Gustav Salling. She must have made many, many visits to her river of birth. *SSG*

Top On 13 June 1958 miserable fishing quotas have forced a number of Shields herring trawlers to lie up in spaces vacated by redundant staiths inside Tyne Dock. *Polar Prince* is prominent, a 1915 product of Eltringham's yard at Willington Quay. A solitary man inspects a dreary scene amidst the North East drizzle. *SSG*

Middle Early in 1959 *North Devon* prepares for the annual race to become the first vessel to arrive at Hudson Bay after the winter ice has melted. She seems to be the recipient of two contributors, with the coaster *Iberian Coast* alongside. Sutherland Quay and Jarrow Slake are behind, and little St Paul's church of St Bede fame is just discernible above the sheds. *JJ*

Bottom Chief Engineer John Ure, in reviewing his next step in re-profiling the river in 1859, decided to '. . .protect the river slopes by high-water stone-facings, except at Jarrow Slake and Coble Dene where existing sand slopes remain. . .' Thus the fate of this area was sealed and the 1845 plans of the York & Newcastle Railway for a dock were eclipsed.

The 'sands' of 1859 were eventually to become mud flats and evolved into timber wet-seasoning 'ponds' on a scale only rivalled in Scandinavia. At high tide and full, the ponds resembled a gently undulating wooden platform. Local children used to run and skip across the timbers up to the distant edge of the river – unafraid of the dangers! This view is dated March 1962, and today this area is part of the Tyne Coal Terminal. *JJ*

Above This is the grand view from the top of the Grain Warehouse overlooking the operations heartland at the eastern side of Tyne Dock in the 1950s. From here could be seen a large part of the 215 acres for the storage of timbers. The inside dock water area was 49 acres, and the LNER was once very proud of the Dock's record shipping achievements, not to mention the boasted 'quickest dispatch for colliers taking coal in the Country'. This was measured in hours – not days! The dock gates are glimpsed with their three entrance canals at 60, 70 and 80 feet widths. *JJ*

Below A picture that sums up Tyne river life and the North East of England in its industrial age (1840-1983) – coal staiths, steam tugs, flat-iron colliers, and the requisite amount of smoke and steam. It may not be suitable calendar fodder, but the loss today of such activity has left the area devoid of certain elements of raw beauty involving man's inventive use of nature's elements, and all the dangers that go with them! We are fortunate to have such pictures to remind us of the way it was. The *Chessington* was built in 1946 to serve Wandsworth Power Station in London. She wasn't seen any more on the river after 1966 after being sold to a Swedish company. *JJ*

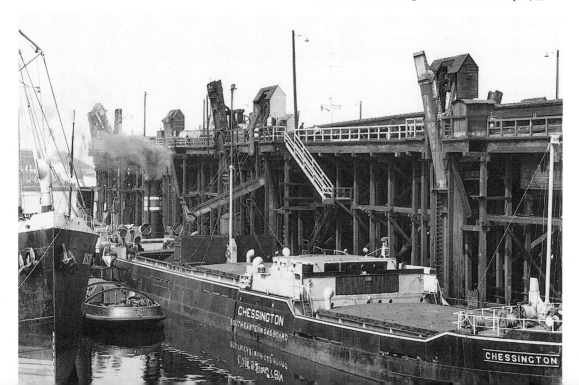

A Tyne book cannot avoid a mention of Tyneside's leading shipping agents, Stephenson, Clarke, owners of many ships special to Tyneside. Their *Broadhurst* is here locked into a tight Tyne Dock at 'A' Staith. Built in 1948 at Grangemouth, she ended her days at Bolckows, Blyth, in 1968. Behind her is the *Avisbrooke*, built at William Gray's yard at Hartlepool in 1943 as the *Empire Harmony*; she ended her time as the *Capetan Panaos* at Piraeus in 1969. Adjacent is *Wanda*, dating back to 1897. She was built as the *Skanderborg*, receiving her new name in 1933; in 1955 she became the *Ridal* and went for scrap as such in 1958, 61 years young.

In the centre background, with a white band on her funnel, is the *Gudrun*. She was built at Kiel in 1924 for Torm's of Copenhagen, and was renamed *Gudrun Torm* in 1951 for an interesting reason. The Danish authorities were tired of the confusion being caused by so many Danish ships carrying the same female name, and decreed that a Christian name must be accompanied by another name to qualify it – hence *Gudrun Torm*. SSG

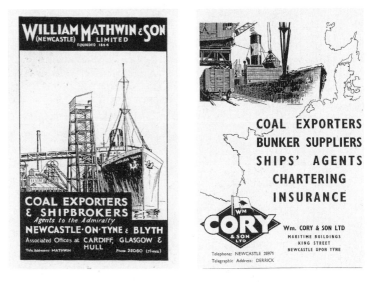

Above Tyne Dock's most easterly staith, 'D' Staith, is occupied on both sides in this 1958 view. The teeming of minerals into the vessels *Johan Jeansson* (left) and *Norfolk Trader* is momentarily interrupted, and it can be seen that teemers are at work with picks attempting to break up possibly baked 'duff' (dusty) coal in a high-sided ex-NER hopper wagon. *JJ*

Left Another of the more rarely seen difficulties that once faced dock workers prior to the age of containerisation was ensuring complete removal of the commodities in a ship's hold, enough to ensure that cleaning was made easy for the next substance, perhaps of a vulnerable nature, to avoid contamination. The hold itself had to be free of glitches to facilitate a clean sweep; a damaged hold has more than once incapacitated a vessel – expensive damage. Here a mini-bulldozer assists the grab cranes at Tyne Dock in recovering iron ore from the Swan Hunter-built carrier *Ruth Lake* in November 1957. *JJ*

Above On 23 April 1973 another piece of the once extensive staiths within Tyne Dock comes crashing down, victim to explosive charges. The original newspaper caption tells us that divers and explosives came courtesy of Precision Blasting of Washington, and adds that divers were making several dives a day to attach charges to the base of the hardwood jetty piles. It seems that the jetty was being blown up in sections of four to five piles at a time. The last operational day of coal shipments had been six years earlier, in March 1967. *SSG*

Below At the height of mining activity circa 1920 the collieries of Northumberland and Durham demanded new pit props at the rate of 10,000 a day. Even though the 1950s saw only half of that number, the demand for props was still extraordinary and led to the continued use of a vast timber business all around the Tyne Dock area. Barely a day passed without a timber boat coming into view off the Tyne Piers bound for Tyne Dock. It also seems that Pyman Bell's timber yard has suffered a collapse on the crane road. The inevitable and ubiquitous 16-ton mineral wagons happen to be a perfect width for the commodity. *JJ*

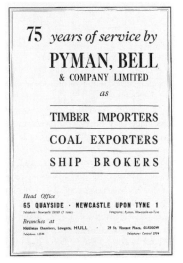

Above left This purpose-built ore quay outside Tyne Dock was designed to give a deeper berth for the midi-ore carriers of 1950s design. The ore gantry gave easy overhead loading into the trains of eight or nine wagons, each capable of 56 tons, which manfully struggled up to Consett until the late 1970s. No longer supplying ore to Consett by the time of this 1979 view, Sutherland Quay had become a multi-purpose facility. *UN*

Left The ore grabs are hard at work on the contents of the *Torne*. Built in 1959 to carry ore for a Swedish company, she became the *Tornado* in 1970 after conversion to an oil carrier for Finnish owners. This view affords a close view of the Stothert & Pitt crane gear. *SSG*

Above Railway-inspired architecture such as this was once seen in hundreds of other locations where large storage facilities were imperative, and the Tyne was no exception. This is the NER's Tyne Dock warehouse with decking quay in the foreground as seen in the mid-1950s. *JJ*

A major bulkhead towards the stern of
the MV *Nigaristan* is lowered
cautiously into place at the yard of John
Readhead & Sons, South Shields, just
downstream of Tyne Dock, in 1947.
Each rib and plate has the part number
chalked on, like some huge
construction kit. The *Nigaristan* went
on to trade for F. C. Strick & Co of
London.

The *Nigaristan*, like so many others
at this time, proudly displayed the Red
Ensign of the British merchant fleet. It
is therefore a sobering thought that as
this book went to print the latest
figures showed that the number now
representing our country abroad has
fallen to 226 (a number that the Tyne,
Wear and Clyde combined could once
produce in a single busy year). *SLL*

6. NORTH AND SOUTH SHIELDS

'Dirty British Coaster with a salt-caked smoke stack,
Butting through the channel in the mad March days,
With a cargo of Tyne coal, road-rail, pig-lead,
Firewood, iron-ware, and cheap tin trays.'

(from 'Cargoes' by John Masefield)

The early growth of salt-making at South Shields is presumed to be connected with easily exploited coal measures. There are references to salt pans in 1499, but it was in the 17th century that we learn how intense the business was, when a contemporary traveller reported: '. . . at Sheeldes . . . I viewed the salt-works and more salt made than in any part of England I know. . .'

A century later, in 1750, a map-maker commented: '. . . South Shields, the station of the sea coal fleets, is a large village eminent for its saltworks, here being upwards of 200 pans for boiling the sea water into salt. . .'

Even then, shipbuilding was making its presence felt, and in Amy Flagg's book we are told: '. . . the eastern extremity of the old township of South Shields was the birthplace and for long the nursery of shipbuilding in our town. . .'

She may as well have been referring to the Tyne in general, for shipbuilding arrived here early in time, and the slipways that Amy refers to are shown on our map in their approximate location, bearing in mind the inaccuracy of early maps. She managed to trace the history of this area from 1729 through to 1919 and says that its history 'is practically serial'. There were many shipbuilders that had a relatively short life in the trade, such were its fluctuations; here is a summary of some examples from her book: William and Catherine Forster c1773-91; James Evens & Son 1788-1831; John Wright 1773-1803; Attley, Swan & Brown 1803-08; J. & P. Laing 1818-30 (better known on Wearside); and Thomas W. Wawn 1846-52. Some

were longer lasting: J. P. Rennoldson & Son 1863-1929; John Readhead & Co 1872-1968; Hepple & Co 1899-1924; Thomas Forsyth & Co 1806-58, H. S. Smith Edwards, 1856-99; and Simon Temple & Son, 1780-1810. This last-mentioned company was one of those successful in wresting the monopoly in naval construction away from the South, and also brings us an interesting story. . .

Simon Temple had a yard 'somewhere in Holborn' with another at the eastern docks, or a predecessor of the Tyne Dock Engineering Company. The first mention of the firm's naval connection comes in 1799. On almost every ship he failed to meet the agreed delivery date for the Admiralty, and it can only be assumed that he was penalised. In spite of this, Temple's son continued to receive naval patronage. In 1806 we learn of the sad fate of their last (and possibly finest) product. She was the 36-gun frigate *Saldanha*. Launched on 8 December 1809 she was lost with nearly all her crew, including the Commander, the Hon William Pakenham, at Lough Swilly off the coast of Ireland on 4 December 1811. She had the best of material lavished upon her, and, Amy tells us, '. . . her loss was one of the prime factors of his downfall'. It appears that his reputation went down with her!

The famous Smith's Dock Company, dating from 1756, is found on this section of the river. This yard opened about 1850 and amalgamated with the Edwards family firm at the turn of the century to form what was primarily the North East's biggest ship-repairing facilities until 1990. Further east still is the Fish Quay and what North Shields is perhaps best known for – kippers. The area was once dotted with the distinct smell from the curing houses.

The high ground above the Union Quay is the site today of the Stag Line Office, now being incorporated within a high-class urban property reconstruction, but the Stag legend continues to shine out to all passing shipping as another memory of when signs of local maritime management involvement was everywhere. Still standing high above and overlooking the sullen Black Midden rocks are Knotts Flats – a sort of smaller 1950s precursor to the 1970s Byker Wall!

Clifford's Fort beyond, although dating back to the 17th century, was used to defend the river as recently as the Second World War, and the Fort is

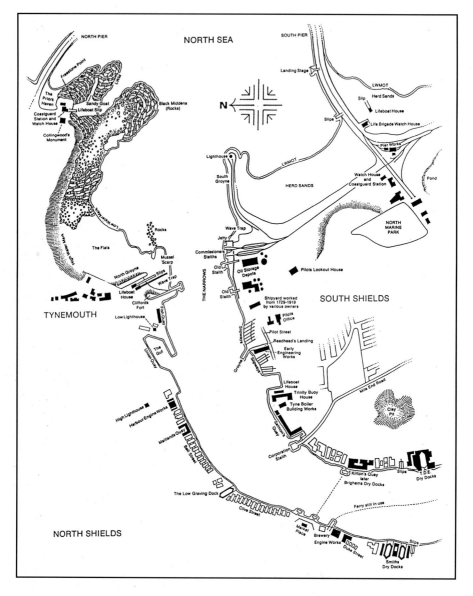

Above The Tyne: North and South Shields

Right South Shields waterfront is spread out before us in this early 1960s view from above the Middle Dock & Engineering Company's dry dock complex that dominated much of the riverside area. In their far dock is *Southern Harvester*, while outside in the river is sister ship *Southern Venturer*, both huge factory whaling ships of the sort much frowned upon by the majority of the world today. Gas, Light & Coke vessels are everywhere, either for repairs or coal loads. East Holborn is prominent, running into Coronation Street. Factories lie on each side of Nile Street, while the busy Commercial Road threads through the railway and factory sites. Further on, the unmistakable hump-backed bridge in Marine Drive is alongside the Brigham & Cowan dry docks. A sad footnote is that these docks were seen being filled in by bulldozers in October 1997. We have to be grateful that such views help us to keep all our memories of a busier Shields alive. *SSG*

almost in line with one of the most important safety aids to early mariners – the Low and High Lighthouses. When vessels approached from the sea a safe entrance past the lurking Black Midden rocks was assured as long as they kept the lights in line. Many, beaten by the weather, looked to the Coastguard as their last chance, but sadly a great many perished, as seen in the illustration of the *Rupert* shipwreck.

Shields may yet again become an excellent viewpoint for river comings and goings as it is well recognised that the decline in the river economy has now 'bottomed out'. As mentioned elsewhere, A. & P. Appledore is leading the way in large vessel repair work, and as we went to press it was learned that the Tyne has been provisionally chosen as the cruise base for the liner *Empress of Canada*, which, like Shearer, is coming home! (She was launched at Vickers-Armstrong's yard in 1964.) A figure of around £65 million has been discussed as the overall cost to facilitate the venture and, *if* it happens, it will certainly represent a massive attraction to the region as the starting point for large numbers of people from all points of the compass. The 'Empress' will more than likely be moored somewhere along the North Shields foreshore, as a ship of this size would now struggle to get safely beyond Walker. She would be a welcome revival to the once familiar 'big ship' presence, but let's simply hope that all goes well, that funding is available and that some local people get work with her.

Whatever occurs, the signs are that Shields' star is once again in the ascendancy!

Above This broad river view from near the Mill Dam, South Shields, affords a wonderful glimpse into the past. On the extreme left is Smith's Docks, which also had facilities on the Tees. To the right is Brigham's dry dock. Centre stage is the Gas, Light & Coke steam collier *Fireside*, awaiting a berth at Harton Staiths, together with *Dulwich* and another. *Fireside* was built on the Wear by S. P. Austin to serve London's firesides with Tyne coal. She did this job until 1962 – two years after this scene – when she was bought by Panamanians who renamed her *Dynamikos*. In 1965 she became the *Nikos V* but was wrecked in 1967.

On the right a TIC dredger is working with a steam hopper, while a gaggle of tugs fuss around *Border Laird*, built in 1955 and managed by Common Brothers for Lowland. *SSG*

Below Smith's Docks of North Shields was well advertised to passing trade and also well respected throughout the world for its high-quality workmanship. This was borne out by the multi-national display of flags that presented an excellent variety for observers on the ferry. Many ships were repaired here, but an advert in the Port of Tyne handbook of 1948 presents Smith's as builders of 'Self-trimming colliers, Oil tankers, Timber carriers, Coasters, Whalers, Trawlers and Tugs', not a bad variety. This view shows *Tiderange* inside, and *Angola* (Hawthorn, Leslie, 1948) and *British Princess* lined up outside. *JJ*

Right One particular dry dock on easy public view was Brigham's Yard, South Shields, overlooked from River Drive, which skirted the riverfront in a wide half circle. The dock entrance was passed by the ferries at the opposite end. Beyond the *Aulica* and over the river at Smith's Docks is the tanker *Caltex Copenhagen* in this early 1960s view. *JJ*

Below Brigham & Cowans graving dock, with its peripheral equipment, is seen from River Drive, South Shields, on a dismal 22 October 1963.

Smith's Docks opposite includes *Brisbane Star* in the queue for attention. *SSG*

Up until the completion of the Tyne Road Tunnel in 1967, those elderly 'characters' the Shields ferries held sway for quick transits between the two towns, and replaced ferries that went back to the 14th century and possible beyond. Motor vehicles were first carried in 1911, and there was always the choice of 'the great way around' or this hop for a few pence more. Although it can be seen that space was at a premium, it must be remembered that the traffic demand was very much lighter, and many even opted to go as pedestrians via the ferry and leave the car. The vessels' demise was inevitable, not only due to their size but also because for 37 years they endured crossings, bumpings and bangings that all left their mark. The present-day service, with *Shieldsman* and *Pride of the Tyne*, caters for cyclists and pedestrians and still affords an albeit brief feel for conditions on the river, although now bereft of vessels huddled up here and there.

The first picture is of *Northumbrian*, built in 1930 by Hawthorn Leslie & Co for the TIC. Next is *Tynemouth* of 1925 vintage, from the yard of Philip & Sons, Dartmouth, and finally *South Shields*, with the taller funnel and the oldest of the trio. She was a product of Wood Skinner & Co of Bill Quay in 1911. It is noticeable that each have detail differences, and no doubt those who manned them over the years also had their favourites. *All JJ*

Above Time was when a journey on the Shields ferry wasn't simple, especially when the many craft off Smith's Docks presented something of a navigational challenge! On 19 September 1973 ferryboat *Freda Cunningham* scrapes her way past two Cunarders, *Franconia* and *Carmania*, both laid up awaiting sale to Russian interests. Both were built at John Brown's famous Clyde yard in the 1950s for Canadian services from Liverpool. On an October 1997 trip not one active ship was on view in this area; if ferry trips are now less hazardous, they are also certainly devoid of atmosphere. *SSG*

Right The ferry landing at South Shields itself is a floating pontoon that rises and falls with the tide. However, its link with terra firma didn't, which used to create the problems, as seen here, with an exceptional high tide. On 20 March 1961 a Northern Laundry collection van swims ashore from the link span after the crossing from North Shields. *JJ*

Above The Tyne had a great tradition of building aircraft carriers that served their country especially well. Perhaps one of the best known, and a ship that led to this great tradition, was the first purpose-built aircraft carrier, HMS *Hermes*. She was built by Armstrong-Whitworth in 1924 and completed at HM Dockyard Devonport. This photograph witnesses the end of this tradition as Swan's Yard No 109 unceremoniously edges out of the Tyne and past the North Shields ferry landing while on trials in December 1984. She is HMS *Ark Royal* and we see her in a low wintry light that perhaps perfectly reflects the evening of our river's great adventure with such perfect creations. *By kind permission of Sirkka-Liisa Konttinen*

Below With the increasing demand for clubman's ales, the Federation Brewery purchased a large new site at Dunston in 1976. Seven new stainless steel fermenting vats are seen arriving in the river in June 1977 to make the journey to Dunston for offloading, where they joined another 14 vats already delivered; getting 28-feet-high vats to Dunston by road would have had its difficulties! Constructed in Kent, the capacity of each was 1,000 barrels, or 288,000 pints! The new brewery opened in the spring of 1979. *SSG*

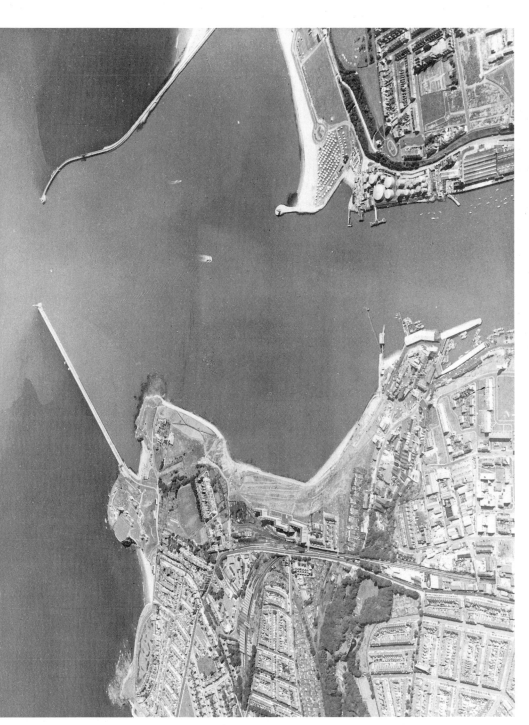

It is difficult now to imagine a Tyne without its piers, but easy to imagine how the Herd Sands 'trap' (middle right) used to lure many ships to their death before the advent of these great guarding 'arms'. The Black Midden rocks also lie docile beneath a high tide towards the left-hand inner bay below the snaking Knotts Flats construction. Tynemouth (left) is laid out before us on either side of the former NER coast route, and North Shields Fish Quay under the white shed roofing appears to be having a quiet moment. *UN*

Left On 20 January 1963 the *Adelfotis II* was outward bound from the Tees to Scotland when a steering problem forced her to come into the Tyne for attention and shelter. An easterly gale blew up and she ran on to the south side of the Groyne at South Shields. These two views depict her situation. All 23 crew were happily taken off by breeches-buoy (as shown in the first picture) under the supervision of the South Shields & Sunderland Life Brigade. She was well photographed thereafter as she lay beached here for some time until she was broken up on site. *SSL*

Right A sombre time that catches humanity at its most ghoulish. A crowd gathers at a safe distance from the wrecked *Rupert* to filch anything of interest that she jettisons during her last moments while breaking up on the notorious Black Midden rocks off Tynemouth in c1880. Her crew would most likely have been saved by rockets launched by the volunteer lifeboatmen of the day. *NCL*

Above left Situated between a breakwater and the Lifeboat Station at North Shields was the often unnoticed Hailing Station provided by Lloyds Shipping Agency, which recorded traffic movements into and out of the Port to satisfy legal requirements and to wire out destinations and safe arrivals to those with an interest, such as owners, agents and the relatives of those at sea. The first view is that presented to ships' masters having, hopefully, negotiated the rocks off Tynemouth. The tannoy, visible, would sing out the request for identity. *JJ*

Above right This is the view from the Station, featuring a vessel being hailed by the officer of the watch. A failure to report satisfactorily would lead to a visit from the River Police – just another aspect of river life that has now disappeared into the maritime history books. *JJ*

Below With the Low Lighthouse (1808) in exact alignment for a healthy arrival into the Tyne we see the protected anchorage at North Shields Fish Quay and the many sheds connected therewith in March 1960. Once famous as the target for hundreds of Scottish 'smokie' herring drifters, the 'kipper' itself was credited to a Tynesider called Woodger, but we will never know for certain. Curing houses still exist, albeit on a tiny scale compared with the Victorian era when many hundreds of women were the mainstay of this once travelling industry, all along the entire East Coast. *JJ*

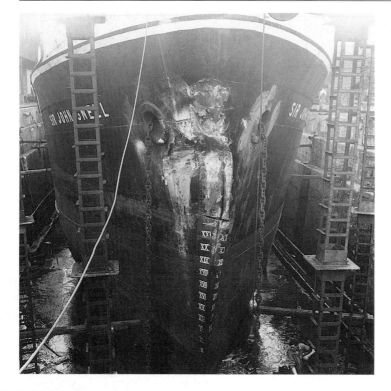

Left A view of *Sir John Snell*'s bloodied nose after his quarrel with the South Pier in August 1959. Commissioned in 1954 especially to trade between the coal ports and Brighton 'B' Power Station, she was designed to be narrow enough to pass the entrance lock at Shoreham. Launched from Hall, Russell's Aberdeen yard in 1955, she spent most of her 25 years trading under the CEGB flag until she ended her days at San Esteban de Pravia breakers, Spain. *JJ*

Below The damage caused by *Sir John*'s attempted short cut is seen here being attended to. The collision loosened several pier blocks, and the crane, part of the original construction equipment, was pressed into service assisted by the diminutive Ruston shunting engine plus purpose-designed wagons of an antique lineage. The small 'railway' on the crane itself and the Morris Minor car complete an interesting tableau.

The piers were begun in 1854 in order to reduce the number of wrecks on both the Herd Sands and the Black Middens. Both ready in 1895, the North Pier was breached by storms in 1897, and was not finally completed until 1909. *JJ*

Journey's end: the mouth of the Tyne in 1960. Collingwood's Monument stands behind the Priory and Castle. *UN*

INDEX